POETIC RAYS:
Visionary and Magnetic

T0099861

POETIC RAYS:
Visionary and Magnetic

—⁂———

KEITH TYRONE BUSH

Order this book online at www.trafford.com
or email orders@trafford.com

www.Createspace.com

Most Trafford titles are also available at major online book retailers.

© Copyright 2011 keith tyrone bush.
All rights reserved. No part of this publication may be reproduced, stored in a retrieval
system, or transmitted, in any form or by any means, electronic, mechanical, photocopying,
recording, or otherwise, without the written prior permission of the author.

Available from Amazon.com
Createspace.com and directly from author:
E-mail: Khnemu@Yahoo.com
Cell #: (203-993-7723)

Printed in the United States of America.

ISBN: 978-1-4269-8191-3 (sc)
ISBN: 978-1-4269-8192-0 (e)

Trafford rev. 09/07/2011

www.trafford.com

North America & International
toll-free: 1 888 232 4444 (USA & Canada)
phone: 250 383 6864 ♦ fax: 812 355 4082

DEDICATION

I dedicate this book to the memory of all of my deceased family members and friends. I dedicate it in particular to my father, Francis Raymond Bush, and those who have just recently passed on in 2008: Richard "Uncle Wee" Bush, William "Uncle Will" Bush III, and cousin Lawrence "Lucky" Bush.

To those bad, bad nieces of mine who have forced their way into my life to become the major tiny vital pulses that keep my heart beating with joy: Tymajee Bush, Najla Bush, the Jones/Bush girls: Tyiona, Tajae, Teniya, Tamia and Da'mhani Yearwood. I also dedicate this book to my patiently awaited niece, not yet born, but is on the way.

This book is equally dedicated to my nephews: Mark "Quick" Elliott, Keith "Weefy" Bush, Travon "Budda man" Jones, and Cody Blackwell, the youngest of my direct bloodline.

This is a special dedication to two of my nephews Mark Bush and Dion Bush. They are currently incarcerated and are pursuing their own challenge to maintain sanity in an abnormal environment. Stay focus and strong! I know you know we draw from the same source of capacity.

To all of my family members, "the Bush and Belle" tribe, and close family friends. There are just too many to name in a lifetime.

To all members of the Resurrection Study Group/The National Trust. Some of them have contributed under the section "Tribute to the Comrades: May I Share Some With You."

Lastly, to Brittnee Burke and Brandon Biscegelia for their assistance in editorial and/or cover design input.

TABLE OF CONTENTS

GREETINGS

RELATIONSHIP

SPIRITUALITY

INNOCENCE

CULTURAL RESURRECTION

INDEX

AUTHOR'S COMMENTS

Without the advice of a few family members this book would not be possible. Putting my poetry into book form was simply not in my interest. If it were up to me, these poems would have remained buried within the paperwork of my files and eventually lost to history. All of my poems were written while in prison except for a recent poem I revised "In Remembrance of Michael Jackson" and a second poem entitled, "And The Theologian Responded." I included a few articles I wrote for your consumption as well. Unlike my poetry, the articles were distributed.

Poetry writing is one of my most intimate forms of expression. The poems you are about to read come directly from my heart. In essence, they mirror my feelings and emotions captured at different stages of my l-o-n-g and harsh 32 years of incarceration. Initially, I wrote poetry to escape prison madness and to release that suppressed part of myself longing for internal expression. Out of this longing I developed a soothing thirst for poetic expression. It gave me a healthy outlet and inner fulfillment that helped ease my wounded spirit.

Writing poems also helped release my personal conflicts. I used poetry as a way to discharge my rage and bitterness. In doing so, I discovered how these negative demons had tried to enslave my humanity. Thanks to this unique form of writing, I learned what leads to hatred and how hatred can cloud rationality. My hatred was the result of hurt/pain that grew out of my experience of injustice.

The topic regarding relationship and the section that pertains to my innocence are highly personal. They are based upon my prison experience and the many years I encountered longing for intimacy. I have included them for no other reason other than what my emotions were and how the impact of living inside of a cage for so many years affected and shaped my mind. They are not for your sympathy. I am including these particular poems with the hope that they will encourage you to value the opportunities you have at your disposal. These opportunities are so often taken for granted if you have never lost your freedom.

The section on cultural identity relates to an important awakening process in my life. Learning African-American/Native American culture, gave me a solid foundation and helped to shape my view of the world. Initially, it was hard digesting the pain endured by my ancestors/elders as they struggled (and continue to) to change those ugly realities of the past and today's discriminatory practices. Fortunately, thanks to the courageous minds of today, past harsh mistreatments are slowly continuing to dissipate. Like the section on innocence, my cultural poems may also appear as too boldly expressed or distastefully raw. Since it is the reality of my past and my experience is the product thereof, I make no apologies. I give no explanations!

Poetry showed me a creative aspect of myself and served as a kind of therapy. In writing poems, I contemplated the inner contour of my psyche. I drew from my information bank, impulses, intuition and night/day dreams of things that came to me. Intuitively, I tried to capture the inner dynamics of what lies deep within my soul. I searched for the God concept, the essence of the soul and collective human drama of which we all play a part. In this fascinating pursuit, I glimpsed an untapped region and found a hidden treasury of precious data preserved from what seemed like life's lessons, stored by some of my soul's past personalities from other places and times. These poems you are about to read are miniscule in proportion to what I have embarked upon in my encounter with the demonic forces that hide deep within the inner dimensions of one's darkest hours of confinement.

Here, I give them to you in appreciation for the inner vitality and fulfillment they gave to me. I know these poems and articles will do as much for you as they have for me. Just think of them as a sprinkle of tiny insight emerging out of the creativity of my **SOUL!!!**

AND SINCE THIS TREASURY WAS
MEANT TO BE FOUND AND TOLD
MAY I PERMEATE WITHIN
YOU AND FOREVER UNFOLD

KEITH TYRONE BUSH

THE POET

LISTEN VERY CAREFULLY AS THE POET
EXPLAINS LIFE'S PROFOUNDEST JOY AND PAIN
MIXED EMOTIONS CAPTURED BY INSIGHT
ARTICULATED WITH SENSITIVITY, PRIDE OR SHAME

THE 'MOTHER FUCK IT' ATTITUDE
EXPRESSED NOT BY WHAT THE POET
ASSUMES BUT BY WHAT THE POET CLAIMS

LISTEN VERY, VERY CAREFULLY TO THE BEAUTY
OF POETIC WISDOM COMPOSED INTO RADIANT SOUNDS
OF RHYTHM THAT ONLY A TRUE POET CAN ARRANGE

LISTEN VERY CAREFULLY TO THE UNIQUE RECITATION OF
THIS POETIC WISDOM, BECAUSE IT WILL NEVER SOUND
THE SAME

HEAR THE APPRECIATION OF THE AUDIENCE
AS THEIR APPLAUSE ERUPTS IN EXCHANGE

THEN LIKE A POWERFUL THUNDER IN HEAVY RAIN
SOMEONE JUMPS FROM THEIR SEAT AND SHOUTS:

"YOW, THAT WAS DEEP!"

SIMULTANEOUSLY, THE POET SMILES WITH A BOW
AS HE BATHES IN A **VAINGLORIOUS MOMENT OF FAME**!

GREETINGS

SPECIAL TRIBUTES ARE FOR SPECIAL PARENTS

DADDY:

YOU SHINE LIKE THE SUN, YOUR GUIDANCE IS AN INFLUENTIAL LIGHT
LIKE A LAMP IN MY HEAD, IT COMES ON LIKE NATURAL INSIGHT
YOU KEPT ME IN LINE AND TAUGHT ME THE THINGS THAT WERE RIGHT
I USED ALL THAT YOU GAVE ME AND FOUND MY PURPOSE IN LIFE

OH, MOMMIE:

ONLY YOU CAN SYMBOLIZE THE ROOT OF A POWERFUL OAK TREE
ONLY YOU HAVE THE GIFT TO TURN LOVE INTO FRUIT BEARING SEEDS
ONLY YOU HAVE THE POWER TO NURTURE WHEN IT IS TIME TO BREED
THANKS FOR TAKING A SEED AND MAKING A BEING OUT OF ME

   *   *   *   *   *   *

YOU BOTH

ARE LIKE AIR AND WIND COMBINED INTO A STRONG
MOVING BREEZE CAUSING OUR FAMILY TREE
TO BLOW, SHAKING BRANCHES AND ALL
OF ITS LEAVES, LIKE A RIPE FRUIT I
CAME LOOSE, YOU KNEW IT WAS
TIME TO FALL FREE, TO
BEGIN MY OWN
JOURNEY

AND ADD TO OUR RICH LEGACY

THANKS FOR ALL THAT YOU GAVE ME AND
THE WISDOM THAT HELPED ME TO SEE

THANKS FOR SHOWING ME THE RIGHT WAY
AND INSTILLING YOUR VALUES IN   ME

THANKS FOR TREATING ME SO SPECIAL
AND   FULFILLING MY SPIRITUAL NEEDS

**I WILL HONOR YOU LIKE GODS, AND RE-CREATE
YOU THROUGH THE BIRTH OF MY SEEDS**

MOMMIE

YOU ARE THE GODDESS OF MY LOVE
THE MISTRESS OF MY SOUL

YOUR HEART IS SWEETER THAN THE SWEETEST
STRONGER THAN THE STRONGEST

MORE DELECTABLE THAN TASTE
MORE GENUINE THAN GOLD

YOUR PERFORMANCE OF MOTHERHOOD IS BEYOND TRUE NAMING
YOU STOOD BEFORE DEATH SO THAT I COULD LIVE
YOU ARE THE FIRST LADY IN MY WORLD

**THUS – IN YOUR NAME – I PROMISE
I WILL HONOR AND RESPECT
EVERY WOMAN AND GIRL**

REMEMBERED FOREVER
HAPPY EARTH DAY DAD

ALTHOUGH YOU HAVE PASSED AWAY
THIS IS STILL YOUR **SPECIAL DAY**

TO YOU DAD:

TO WHOM I HAVE HAD THE GREATEST
PLEASURE TO KNOW, INFLUENCED BY
THE DESIRE TO BE STRONG LIKE YOU,

I DEVELOPED THE CAPACITY TO SURVIVE

TO A MIGHTY, MIGHTY WARRIOR
NOW PHYSICALLY DECEASED
BUT IN MY HEART

YOU WILL NEVER DIE !

IN REMEMBERANCE OF MICHEAL JACKSON

HIS ABILITIES AND TALENT IN SONG AND DANCE DAZZLED US WITH AMAZE
HIS HUMANITARIAN SERVICE LEFT HIS FRINGERPRINTS ON THE WORLD'S STAGE
THE DISHEARTENING SHOCKING NEWS OF HIS SUDDEN DEATH LEFT US IN A DAZE

OH, BUT WHAT A RIGHTEOUS INVESTMENT HE MADE

HIS CARING AND GIVING CONTAINED AS MUCH IN
SERVICE AS THE MANY GOOD DEEDS CONTAINED
WITHIN A RIGHTEOUS INVESTMENT– IT WAS LIKE:

FINDING THE ANSWER TO THE ULTIMATE QUESTION THAT
STIMULATES THE PSYCHE AND KEEP US ALL GUESSING

USING THE EARTH AS A TRAINING GROUND
FOR OUR OWN PERSONAL TESTING

TO FIND TRUTH ON OUR JOURNEY AND
TO LEARN FROM LIFE'S LESSONS

TO MANIFEST ON JUDGMENT DAY
OUR MOST INTIMATE CONFESSIONS

**FOR HIS SERVICES OF ENTERTAINMENT AND GOOD DEEDS,
TO GOD, MY CONFESSION READS:**

HE SERVED TO MAKE THE WORLD
BETTER AND BECAME ONE OF OUR
PRECIOUS EARTHLY BLESSINGS

PLEASE BATHE HIS SOUL IN
YOUR SPIRITUAL ESSENCE

SIBLING RIVALRIES

TOGETHER   THIS IS A SONG DEDICATED TO THEE, SISTERS AND BROTHERS WITH FOND OR PAINFUL MEMORIES. WHILE THEY PLAY IT, WILL YOU DANCE WITH ME, AND SHOW OUR CHILDREN HOW LOVE PRESERVES OUR FAMILY

FEMALE   I STILL REMEMBER THE DAY YOU WERE BORN, CUDDLE JUST RIGHT IN MY DADDY'S WARM TENDER ARMS, IN JEALOUSLY, I FELT SO ALL ALONE. MOMMA LOOKED DOWN AT ME AND KNEW SOMETHING WAS WRONG

SHE KISSED MY FOREHEAD AND WHISPERED TO ME, WHY ARE YOU SAD? INSTEAD YOU SHOULD BE HAPPY. HE'S YOUR BROTHER, WE MADE HIM FOR YOU, SO YOU CAN LOVE HIM THE WAY WE BOTH LOVE YOU

WHEN I FIRST HELD YOU, YOUR HANDS SCANNED MY FACE, BLENDING YOUR SMILE WITH MY CURIOUS INTENSED EMBRACE. FROM THAT MOMENT, YOU BECAME MY BEST FRIEND, A SPECIAL GIFT THAT ONLY GOD COULD SEND

MALE   OF COURSE, SISTER, I WILL DANCE WITH YOU, AND REMINISCE ABOUT ALL THE THINGS WE'VE BEEN THROUGH

DO YOU REMEMBER, WHEN I WOULD SKIP SCHOOL, YOU KEPT IT A SECRET WHEN I WOULD BREAK A FAMILY RULE, YOU HAD MY BACK AND I HAD YOURS TOO, I EVEN FOUGHT AGAINST ALL THE BOYS THAT PICKED ON YOU

WHEN YOU GOT OLDER, YOU HAD YOUR FIRST DATE, YOU WERE SO IN LOVE, YOU THOUGHT DESTINY HAD SEALED YOUR FATE. IN TIME YOU LEARNT JUST HOW SAD LOVE CAN BE, WHEN I GOT REVENGE, YOU GOT MAD AND TOOK IT OUT ON ME

A TERRIBLE SCENE THAT ALMOST LED TO A FIGHT, FROM IT WE LEARNED LESSONS ABOUT WHAT IS WRONG AND RIGHT

FEMALE   OF COURSE, I WOULD LOVE TO DANCE WITH YOU AND REMINISCE ABOUT ALL THE THINGS WE'VE BEEN THROUGH

TOGETHER   IF IT COULD HAPPEN, WE WOULD RE-LIVE IT AGAIN. IF WE COULD DO IT, WE WOULD ERASE ALL OUR PAIN AND SINS, A LIFE OF JOY IS FOR ALL WE WOULD WISH, AND TO SHOW OUR CHILDREN HOW THEY CAN FIND TRUE HAPPINESS

IF FAMILY LOVE IS WHAT YOUR FAMILY MISS, TAKE IT FROM US - LOVE IS THE PERFECT FAMILY GIFT. TO GET IT BACK, WITHOUT TAKING A RISK, JUST SHOW SOME LOVE, AND WATCH YOUR FAMILY FEEL THE BLISS

HUG YOUR BROTHER, GIVE YOUR SISTER A KISS. WE HOPE THIS SONG WILL LEAVE YOU WITH PEACE AND HAPPINESS

THIS IS A SONG – DEDICATED TO THEE BROTHERS AND SISTERS WITH FOND OR PAINFUL MEMORIES, WHILE THEY PLAY IT WILL YOU DANCE WITH ME, AND SHOW OUR CHILDREN HOW LOVE PRESERVES OUR FAMILY

EARTH DAY

ON THIS GLORIOUS DAY YOU IMPRINTED
YOUR MARK UPON THE UNIVERSE

YOU ENTERED THIS WORLD THROUGH THE
WOMB WITH A POWERFUL BURST

JOY FILLED THE AIR AS THE DOCTOR
HANDED YOUR PRECIOUS BODY TO THE NURSE

<u>BUT ON THIS SPECIAL DAY</u>

YOU MUST HONOR **YOUR MOTHER FIRST**
SHE WAS THE ONE WHO GAVE BIRTH
YOU WERE THE ONE WHO ENTERED THE EARTH

**HAPPY BIRTH DAY TO YOUR MOTHER
AND HAPPY EARTH DAY TO YOU**

FAMILY REUNION INVITATION

GATHERING OF THE HARVEST IS FOR
SOCIAL COMMUNION

A COMING TOGETHER IS FOR
FAMILY REUNION

TO ENJOY THE MOMENT AND
HONOR OUR PAST

TO TURN ANOTHER EVENT INTO
MEMORIES THAT WILL LAST

THIS INVITATION IS EXTENDED
FOR THIS SPECIAL OCCASION

WE HOPE YOU WILL ATTEND
WITHOUT ANY HESITATION

THE SHINING STAR

I AM "THE SHINING STAR"
YOU ARE MY GREATEST FAN

PERFORM FOR ME!

YOU ARE A MERE ACTOR AND OR ACTRESS, MUSICIAN, SINGER, RAPPER, DANCER, AN ATHLETE, SEEKING TO EARN MY CLAIM OF FAME – I PLAYED YOUR ROLES IN PAST LIVES, IN THIS LIFE, I AM HERE TO BE ENTERTAINED

PERFORM FOR ME!

TO MEET MY EXPECTATION, YOU MUST PRACTICE ALL THE TIME, ACTORS/ACTRESSES YOU ARE MERE PRETENDERS BECAUSE YOUR ROLES ARE ALREADY DEFINED, BUT THE ROLE I PLAY IS REAL, BECAUSE, IT IS REALLY MINE, AND THE DUES I PAID TO BE THIS STAR, MAKE ME DIVINE

PERFORM FOR ME!

FAILTURE TO MANIFEST YOUR SPECIALIZED GIFT COULD LEAD TO MENTAL ANGUISH OR DISASTER, DON'T YOU SEE, YOUR TASK IS TO MEET MY NEEDS. YOU ARE MY SERVANT, MY TASK IS TO BE PLEASED, BECAUSE I AM YOUR MASTER

PERFORM FOR ME!

WHEN I FEEL LIKE BUGGING, MAKE MY THUGISH BEAT, IF I FEEL LIKE HAVING FUN, MAKE ME MOVE MY FEET, WHEN I FEEL LIKE ROMANCING, SING MY FAVORITE SONGS, WHEN YOU MAKE MY VIDEOS, I WANT ALL THE WOMEN IN THONGS

PERFORM FOR ME!

YOU ARE BLINDED BY THE STAR-LIGHT THAT SHINES UPON YOU YOU ARE MADE LARGER THAN LIFE SO THAT THE PEOPLE CAN FOCUS ON YOU, I DID THAT SO I COULD REMAIN HIDDEN FROM VIEW, DON'T YOU SEE, " I AM THE REAL CELEBRITY, " I USED YOU TO CONCEAL AND PROTECT MY OWN PRIVACY

YOU PERFORM FOR ME!

MAKE A WISH

CLOSE YOUR EYES AND FANTASIZE
A WISH WILL THEN BE SEEN

USE THAT WISH TO VISUALIZE
IT WILL GUIDE YOU TO A DREAM

IF YOU KEEP THAT WISH ALIVE
THAT DREAM WILL NEVER DIE

WHAT YOU SEE IS YOURS TO BE
IT IS ALL RIGHT THERE INSIDE

*   *   *   *

FIND THAT PLACE AND YOU WILL FIND
YOUR FATE, WAITING TO BE OBJECTIFIED

BUT DON'T WAIT TO LATE OR HESITATE
OR THAT DREAM WILL PASS YOU BY

FEED THAT WISH UNTIL IT'S BLISS
AND IT WILL START TO COME ALIVE

BUT DON'T FORGET TO SHARE YOUR
GIFT AND IT WILL SURELY MULTIPLY

BUSH WEAR /730-ORIGINAL

BE PROUD OF THIS GEAR
IT'S MADE BY BUSH-WEAR
THE MASTERFUL DESIGNERS
WITH CREATIVITY THAT RARE

THE PRODUCT OF THIS WORK
IS MULTICULTURAL AND DIVERSE,
SOOTHING YOUR INNER THIRST
WITH INNOVATIVE URBAN GEAR

OR CLASSY CAUSAL GARBS
MADE WITH TENDER CARE

"FOR HUMANITY ONLY"

IS THE TASK WE HOLD DEAR
OUR PATTERNS ARE UNIQUE
OUR STYLES WILL NEVER DISAPPEAR

PEARLS OF THE FASHION WORLD
ARE THE SAME WHEN YOU HERE

**THE MASTERFUL DESIGNERS
MAKERS OF BUSH-WEAR**

RELATIONSHIP

BEAUTY IS PREFERENCE

THERE IS NO SUCH THING AS AN UGLY PERSON
THERE ARE JUST DIFFERENT LOOKING ONES THAN OTHERS
BEAUTY IS ALWAYS BASED ON INDIVIDUAL PERFERENCE
PREFERENCES DIFFER FROM ONE PERSON TO ANOTHER

IT IS THE INTERFACE THAT BLAZES THE HEARTS OF TRUE LOVERS

SOME THINK BEAUTY IS FOUND ONLY IN THE FACE

BUT THAT IS NOT WHERE ALL BEAUTY IS PLACED

THERE IS BEAUTY IN ALL COLORS AND SHAPES

TO DISPLAY AND TO ATTRACT AS BAIT

APHRODISIAC IS THE BEAUTY THAT LOVE MAKES

TO ENSURE THE EXISTENCE OF THE RACE

BEAUTY IS A PRECIOUS GIFT FROM GOD

BLESSED WITH DIVERSIFIED QUALITIES AND TASTE

BEAUTY CAN BE FOUND IN ALL WISDOM

FOR A CONVEYOR THAT LOVE TO CONVERSATE

A PERSONALITY CENTERED IN SPIRITUALITY

CREATES BEAUTY THAT IN/OUTWARDLY RADIATES

THUS, BEAUTY IS NOTHING BUT PREFERENCE

THAT DIFFERS FROM MATE TO MATE

'FOR THOSE WHO SEE UGLINESS OVER PREFERENCE'

'THEIR SIGHT HAS BEEN BLINDED BY SELF-HATE'

MY LOVE

MY LOVE DOES NOT
 COME FROM MY HEART

    MY LOVE COMES FROM
    THE ESSENCE OF MY SOUL

    *   *   *

    WHICH   MUST   NOT   BE
    THAT   FAR   APART

    THAT'S WHY I CAN FEEL
IT   IN   MY   HEART

                AS IT C-O- M-E-S AND G-O-E-S

18

A SPECIAL TRIBUTE TO A SPECIAL WOMAN

DEEP   ROOTED   COMMITMENT
SINCERE   LOYALTY   AND   FAITH

DISPLAYED   FEATURES   OF   STRENGTH,
WISDOM   AND   DIGNITY   UPON   YOUR   FACE

DELECTABLE QUALITIES OF RADIANT BEAUTY AND GRACE
TO ENTICE   WITH   CHARM YOUR   INDIVIDUAL UNIQUENESS

'CONCOCTED WITH BRILLIANCE AND TASTE'

*   *   *   *

CONCEIVED   BY   GOD'S   WILL   UPON   CREATIVITY
EXCESSIVELY BATHED IN THE ESSENCE OF FEMININE DIVINITY

CLOTHED   IN   A   MELANIC   SHADE   LAYER, YOU   ARE
THE   ANSWER   TO   MY   LONG   AWAITED   PRAYER

*   *   *   *

GIFTED   ATTRIBUTES   LIKENED   TO   AN   ANCIENT   QUEEN
FOUNTAIN   STREAMS   OF   PURE   LOVE   AND   SENSITIVITY
SPRINGING   FORTH   MIRACULOUSLY FROM WITHIN YOUR GENES

FROM   YOUR   SOUL   LOVE   FLOWS
LIKE   A   GENTLE   PEACEFUL   STREAM
YOU   ARE   THE MOST PRECIOUS AMONGST

'ALL SPECIES OF WOMB-BEINGS'

*   *   *   *

THANK YOU, ALMIGHTY GOD FOR THE JOY THAT SHE BRING
AND   FOR   THE   BLESSINGS   TO   MY   GLOURIOUS   DREAMS
OH LORD, THANK YOU FOR   THIS   VERY SPECIAL WOMAN

THE JOURNEY RIDE TO HEAVEN

TEMPERATURE FIXED AT A FERVANT 98.6 **'TENDER PINK WALLS'**
PROTECTED BY ARMY FILAMENTS – BENEATH SOFT POWDERED LIPS
COUCHED IN DOUBLE-HOOD LABIA–THE SENSITIVE **MANNEQUIN** SITS
DIRECTING THE JOURNEY TO HEAVEN BY
PENETRATION, TOUCH, KISS, SUCK OR LICK

TO ENTER THE PARADISE OF WOMB USE
FOREPLAY AND SHE WON'T RESIST, IT APPEALS TO THE
WILL OF THE MANNEQUIN WHERE THE HEART OF HER 'PASSION' EXISTS

BETWEEN THE SMOOTH TEXTURE OF HER INNER THIGHS
AN EROTIC SCENT OF APHRODISIAC LIES
GENERATING SPARKS OF PASSIONATE HEAT

HER SEXUAL NATURE TURNS HEAT INTO FIRE GIVING
RISE TO THE **'SEX-GOD MESSIAH'** WHILE
BOTH SEEK TO REACH THE ULTIMATE PEEK

'BODIES BATHING IN LUST AND DESIRE'

THE INTOXICATED AROMA OF AROUSED HOT FLESH COMBINED
BY WARM BODIES - INTERWINED - IN A PERFECT COZY FIT

THE MOANING AND SLURPING SOUNDS OF INTENSED
LOVE-MAKING CAUSED BY RHYTHMIC DANCING HIPS
STIMULATION BUILD-UP AS BODY CHEMISTRIES BLISS
THEN THE POWERFUL CLIMACTIC EXPLOSION
DOWN THE WALLS OF HER WARM UTERUS

AFTER MULTIPLE RAIN STORMS OF
ECSTACY HER BODY THEN
S-L-O-W-L-Y RESISTS, WHILE
RESTING IN DEEP STATES
OF FANTASY

'CREAMY NECTAR CONTINUES TO'

DRIP

DRIP

DRIP

BATHING IN THE NOW

THE NOW: THE PRESENT, RIGHT HERE, THE MOMENT

ONLY IN 'THE NOW' CAN OUR SOULS PEEK THROUGH DIVINITIY'S MORTAL EYES TO VIEW WHAT LIES IN THE PRECIOUS MOMENT

ONLY IN 'THE NOW' CAN WE BEAR WITNESS TO THE SUN'S ASTONISHING BEAUTY AND ITS WARM PENETRATING RAYS, FLICKING DELICATE SILVER AND/OR GOLDEN LIGHT SHOTS UPON THE SURFACE OF THE WAVERY WATERS

'RHYTHMICALLY DANCING, DANCING AND DANCING'

FOR THE NOW

*   *   *   *   *

COME, BATH WITH ME, LET'S MARVEL IN THE SUN'S WARMTH, IN NUDITY

LET'S MAKE LOVE AND FEEL THE NOW'S DEEPEST STATE OF ECSTASY

LET'S ENJOY THE SLURPY ESSENCE OF THE NOW'S SEXUAL LIQUIDITY

LET'S RECORD IT AND LEAVE BEHIND OUR OWN SPECIAL MEMORIES

LET'S DO IT, RIGHT HERE, IN THE MOMENT

FOR THE NOW

LET'S MAKE UP

YOU   CAN   STOP   ME
FROM TALKING TO YOU

YOU CAN MAKE ME
FEEL GUILTY TOO

BUT   THERE   IS   ONE
THING YOU CAN NOT DO

'<u>YOU CAN NOT STOP ME FROM LOVING YOU</u>'

ENJOY YOUR LIFE

ENJOY YOUR LIFE, DON'T FUSS OR FIGHT, IT'S THE WORST PRICE TO PAY
NO ONE KNOWS WHEN DEATH WILL STRIKE AND TAKE YOUR LIFE AWAY

LIVING YOUR LIFE IN CONFLICT, IS SIMPLY NOT THE WAY, DON'T WAIT
TOO LATE TO MAKE-UP, BECAUSE THE MORGUE WILL CALL ONE DAY

I WILL NEVER FORGET THAT DAY ON MY WAY TO THE MORGUE
IT WAS THE WORST NEWS I EVER RECEIVED,
MY SOUL - MATE DIED OF A NATURAL CAUSE

I NEVER REALLY UNDERSTOOD, UNTIL
DEATH MADE ITS CALL. LOOSING THE
ONE I LOVED THE MOST WAS
THE GREATEST PAIN OF ALL

*   *   *   *

THE TIME WILL COME IN EVERY RELATIONSHIP WHEN ONE OF YOU WILL DEPART
BEWARE OF THIS SUDDEN TRAGEDY, IT COULD BREAK YOUR WORLD APART

IT'LL LEAVE YOU TRAPPED IN LONELINESS AND CONSUME YOUR PRECIOUS HEART
EACH MOMENT YOU SHARE IS PRICELESS, SO ENJOY IT FROM THE START

THE LIFE YOU SHARE WILL BE CHERISHED,
OR REMEMBERED FOREVER MORE, MEMORIES
CONTAIN THE CHOICES WE MAKE, SO MAKE
YOUR CHOICES WORTH LIVING FOR

LEAVE ROOM FOR MISTAKES, BUT DON'T
LET IT BREAK THE BOND RELATIONSHIPS
ARE MADE OF, SOME MISTAKES CAN
LEAD TO HATE AND DESTROY
THE BASE OF TRUE LOVE

BEFORE YOU SEPARATE
REMEMBER THIS FATE:

'ONE DAY YOU WILL LOSE YOUR BELOVED'

**IF IT'S PAINFUL 'YOU WILL LEARN' HOW BAD MEMORIES TURN
INTO TEARS THAT FALL LIKE RAIN FROM THE HEAVENS ABOVE**

LUV-TRAYAL

WHEN YOUR LOVE FIRST TOUCHED MY HEART, I FELT SO VERY GLAD
I NEVER THOUGHT LOVE COULD END - OH, SO VERY FAST

THAT DAY YOU LEFT ME FOR SOMEONE ELSE, I FELT SO VERY SAD
YOU WALKED AWAY FROM A PRECIOUS UNION, AND DESTROYED THE LOVE WE HAD

\-   \-   \-   \-   \-

YOU PROMISED TO MAKE ME HAPPY WITH A COZY FAMILY
INSTEAD YOU TURNED MY LOVE FROM JOY, INTO A WORLD OF MISERY

NOW YOU WANT ANOTHER CHANCE, BUT YOU HAVEN'T MADE A CHANGE
A CHANCE TO DRAIN MY FEELINGS, WITH YOUR SAME OLD SILLY GAMES

*   *   *   *   *

**<u>YOU BETRAYED THE COMMAND THAT LOVE DEMANDS,
YOU STAINED MY HEART WITH PAIN</u>**

*   *   *   *   *

WHY DOES LOVE FEEL SO GOOD, THEN HURT SO VERY BAD?

HOW DO SOME COUPLES REMAIN TOGETHER
AND MAKE THEIR RELATIONSHIPS LAST?

WHY DO MEMORIES REMIND
US OF WHAT WE ONCE HAD?

HOW DO PEOPLE AMEND
THEIR DIFFERENCES
AND LEAVE MISTAKES
IN THE PAST?

WHY MUST WOUNDS
HEAL IN TIME, BEFORE
LOVE CAN SLOWLY MEND?

AND WHY MUST ALL LESSONS
FIRST BE LEARNED BEFORE
THE HEART CAN LOVE AGAIN?

GO AHEAD AND CRY

WHEN SOMEONE YOU DEEPLY LOVE DIES
OR WHEN YOUR HIDDEN FEARS COME ALIVE
BEFORE THE TEARS CAN FLOW YOU
ALWAYS TRY TO HIDE, BECAUSE YOU
BELIEVE STRONG PEOPLE SHOULD NEVER CRY
BUT IF WATER FALLS NATURALLY FROM THE
SKY WHY STOP THE TEARS THAT SEEK THE
SAME EXPRESSION THROUGH YOUR EYES?
DAMN, WHAT A RIDICULOUS PRIDE,
YOUR EMOTIONS SEEK EXPRESSION
WHILE YOUR FEELINGS TRY TO HIDE,

HAS ANYONE EVER TOLD YOU:

PEACE, COMES AFTER THE TEARS RUN DRY,
AND THE FEAR, IT DISAPPEARS THROUGH
THE PAIN RELEASED FROM INSIDE
FROM THE SOURCE OF NATURE
ALL THINGS CAME, THERE ARE SOME
THINGS IN LIFE SHE PURPOSELY ARRANGED

THE EARTH CANNOT BALANCE
ITSELF WITHOUT THE FALL OF RAIN

NATURE CAN NOT RELEASE ITS NEGATIVE FORCES
WITHOUT EARTHQUAKES, TORNADOES OR HURRICANES

YOUR FAILURE TO RELINQUISH PAIN WILL EVENTUALLY DRIVE YOU INSANE

GO AHEAD AND CRY, UNLOCK THE
SORROW IN YOUR SOUL OR YOUR
TRUE NATURE WILL BE DENIED
LET THE TEARS FALL NATURALLY FROM YOUR EYES
AND DON'T FEEL ASHAMED! REMEMBER THIS:
'PAIN STAINS THE HEART IF NOT DRAINED'

FOR THOSE WHO CLAIM THEY NEVER CRIED
ARE THOSE WHO TELL THE BIGGEST LIES
OR ARE THOSE WHO HURT THE MOST INSIDE

I KNOW BECAUSE AFTER MY TEARS RUN DRY,

'MY HEART FEELS NO PAIN'

LUVMERIZED

THE FIRST TIME I SAW HER, I WAS CAUGHT BY SURPRISE
SHE RAN WAY FROM A FOOLISH MAN, WITH TEARS IN HER EYES

I FELT WHAT SHE WAS GOING THROUGH WHILE I STOOD THERE HYPNOTIZED
I KNEW SHE WAS THE ONE FOR ME, AS SHE RAN PAST MY SIDE

I WANTED TO CATCH AND COMFORT HER, BUT ASSUMED SHE WOULD WALK AWAY,
SO I DECIDED TO LET HER BE ALONE, AND TRY ANOTHER DAY

ONE NIGHT I ATTENDED JUSTIN, A SINGLE MAN WITHOUT A DATE
WHILE LISTENING TO 'THE WHISPERS' PLAYED, I TURN AND SAW MY FATE

THERE SHE WAS, ALL ALONE, THIS TIME I COULD NOT WAIT, WHEN
SHE TURNED AROUND OUR EYES MET, WITH A SMILE ON HER FACE

I WAS LUVMERIZED BY HER BEAUTY, AND OBSERVABLE CLASSY TASTE
SHE WAS DEFINITELY A PERFECT 10, SHE LIT UP THE ENTIRE PLACE

I KNEW FROM WHAT I FELT INSIDE IT WAS TIME TO MAKE MY MOVE, AS I
APPROACHED THE WHISPERS SLOWED IT DOWN AND PUT US IN A GROOVE

I WAS IN A TRANCE, WHEN I REACHED OUT MY HAND AND ASKED HER FOR A
DANCE I EMBRACED HER SAFELY IN MY ARMS, AS IF LOVE HAD JUST BEEN BORN

WHEN I CLOSED MY EYES AND VISUALIZED MY LONELINESS WAS GONE
SHE LAYED HER HEAD UPON MY CHEST WHILE THE WHISPERS SUNG OUR SONG

SECRET ADMIRER

OH, MOTHER NATURE

AT TIMES YOU CAN BE
SO VERY, VERY CRUEL

IF YOU ARE GOING TO
MAKE ME ATTRACTED TO HER

WHY DON'T YOU MAKE HER
ATTRACTED TO ME TOO?

CHOLOCATE COATED CANDY

EAT ME, I TASTE LIKE
CHOLOCATE COATED CANDY

I WANT TO BE YOUR
SWEETEST TASTING FANTASY

THAT CREAM INSIDE ME
WAS DIPPED IN NATURE'S NECTARY

TASTE ME AND MAKE ME
YOUR FINGER LICKING ECSTASY

*   *   *   *

ONE THING YOU SHOULD KNOW
BEFORE YOU PUT YOUR LIPS ON ME

I AM HIGHLY ADDICTIVE
WITH CRAVING DELECTABILITY

TRY ME AND SEE, I
WILL SOOTHE YOUR FEMININITY

THEN MIX ALL MY CHOLOCATE
WITH YOUR CREAMY BODILY CHEMISTRY

PLUCK ME

I WAS THE FIRST RIPE FRUIT
HANGING ON THIS TREE

WAITING JUST FOR YOU TO
COME ALONG AND PLUCK ME

*   *   *

IF YOU DO NOT PLUCK ME I
WILL FALL FROM THIS TREE

LIKE THE OTHERS THAT FELL BEFORE
ME, I WILL SOON CEASE TO BE

*   *   *

I WILL LEAVE BEHIND MY SEED
AND RETURN LIKE DEJA VU

I WILL BECOME A FRUIT AGAIN AND AGAIN
UNTIL I AM FINALLY PLUCKED BY YOU

LOVE DIALOGUE:
BETWEEN A MAN AND WOMAN

MAN: I JUST WANT TO TOUCH YOUR SOUL
I JUST WANT TO BATHE WITH YOU IN PURE LOVE
THEN FILL YOUR HEART WITH PLEASANT MEMORIES
THAT WILL NEVER GROW OLD - MEMORIES THAT WILL
FOREVER UNFOLD

WOMAN: HOW WILL YOU REPLACE THE JOY THAT HE STOLE?
IF YOUR LOVE IS REAL, TELL ME, HOW WILL I KNOW?
AND WHY SHOULD I BELIEVE YOU WHEN EVERYONE KNOWS

THAT NO ONE CAN ACTUALLY 'TOUCH A SOUL'?

MAN: I KNOW THE PLACE WHERE YOUR HEART SHINES LIKE GOLD
THE ENTRANCE AND EXIT WHERE LOVE COMES AND GOES
I WILL FIND ALL YOUR WOUNDS AND SEAL EVERY HOLE
THEN POUR ALL OF MY LOVE ALL OVER YOUR SOUL

WOMAN: I NEED THE KIND OF HAPPINESS THAT ONLY HEAVEN BRINGS
A COMMITTED AND STRONG MAN IS THE HOPE OF MY DREAMS
WHEN I SLEEP ALL ALONE MY LONELINESS APPEARS,
HAUNTING MY SPIRIT WITH SLEEPLESS NIGHTMARES

WILL YOU COMFORT AND HOLD ME WHEN I WAKE UP IN FEAR?
WHEN I CALL OUT YOUR NAME, TELL ME, WILL YOU BE THERE?
WILL YOU CATCH AND GENTLY WIPE AWAY ALL OF MY TEARS?

WILL YOU ALWAYS MAKE LOVE TO ME WITH WARM TENDER CARE?
AND WHEN TIME SEIZES MY YOUTH, WILL YOU STILL BE HERE
LOVING ME UNCONDITIONALLY AND REMAINING SINCERE?

MAN: FROM YOUR 'HEART' TO YOUR 'SOUL'
I WILL CAPTURE THAT SPACE IN BETWEEN
THEN TURN IT INTO A PLEASANT LOVE SCENE

WHEN YOU SLEEP YOU CAN ESCAPE TO THIS ADVENTUROUS STATE
IT'S WHERE 'SOUL-MATES' COMBINE INTO 'LOVE-BEINGS'
I WILL TURN OUR SPIRITS INTO GATES TO PROTECT THIS SPECIAL
PLACE, THEN MAKE LOVE TO YOU FOREVER IN A DREAM

EACH MORNING YOU WILL AWAKE WITH A SMILE ON YOUR FACE
FEELING SEXIER THAN THE SEXIEST OF ALL QUEENS
THEN YOU WILL KNOW THAT I TOUCHED YOUR SOUL
AND MADE US A PERFECT 'LOVE – TEAM'

OH, WHAT A WONDERFUL JOY IT WOULD BRING

DREAM DISTURBANCE

THAT NIGHT I LAY IN MY VACANT BED THINKING ABOUT THE FEELING OF BEING
LOVED UNTIL MY CONSCIOUSNESS WAS SEIZED BY MY DREAMING SELF
USING OUR SPIRIT AS A VEHICLE, IT TOOK ME ON A JOURNEY
'SOMEPLACE NEAR BUT FAR'

SUDDENLY AN ILLUMINATING LIGHT APPEARED, SHINING SO BRIGHT
ITS WARMTH GENERATED A RADIANT GRACE THAT FELT LIKE HEAVEN

MIRACULOUSLY, I FOUND MYSELF IN A SPECIAL PLACE THAT LOOKED FAR
MORE BEAUTIFUL THAN PARADISE, THE SURROUNDING DISPLAYED
AN AMICABLE BLISS ENGULFED BY EASE FAR MORE SOOTHING THAN PLEASURE
THE SCENERY SEEMED TO APPEAR, DISAPPEARED OR RE-APPEAR BY
THE MERE POWER OF WISH, INTENT AND DESIRE

OUT OF NOWHERE – YOU APPEARED BEFORE ME, IN NUDITY, KNOWING
I WOULD ARRIVE – YOUR BODY GAVE OFF A YEARNING SEXUAL AROMA
'LIKE NO OTHER' - TELEPATHICALLY, I WAS HYPNOTIZED BY YOUR
LONGING TO BE FULFILLED SOMEPLACE DEEP INSIDE YOU

IT WAS LIKE READING A SPIRITUAL SIGN THAT MEANT: "ON THIS PLANE,
LOVE-MAKING IS PURELY SACRED AND DIVINE, BUT TO REACH ITS
ULTIMATE PEEK, YOU MUST FIRST MAKE LOVE TO MY MIND"

I REACHED OUT AND HELD YOU IN MY ARMS FOR WHAT SEEMED LIKE
'AN ETERNAL MOMENT.' SIMULTANEOUSLY, THE CREATOR TWINKLED AND
THE MOST INTIMATE FEELINGS OF EXCITATION BEGAN TO SPRINKLE
'ALL OVER OUR GLOSSING BODIES'

I COULD FEEL IT WARMING MY SOUL WITH AN ECSTASY THAT FELT MORE
PLEASURABLE THAN AN ULTIMATE MULTIPLE ORGASM, WITH MY ARMS
FIRMLY AROUND YOU I COULD FEEL OUR SPIRITS INTERTWINING
AND OUR SOULS DANCING IN HARMONY WITH PERFECTION

WE STOOD THERE, EMBRACED IN A SPIRITUALITY TRANCE LOVE STATE
BUT JUST BEFORE OUR SOULS COULD TRANSCEND AND BLISS
INTO GOD'S REALM OF PURE HAPPINESS, I WAS SADLY
DISTURBED BY YOUR HEARTBROKEN WORDS AS YOU
WHISPERED THEM IN MY RIGHT EAR:

" WILL YOU COME BACK TO MEET ME HERE? "

CAUGHT BY SURRISE, I LOOKED DEEP INTO YOUR EYES AS THEY BEGIN TO TEAR
SUDDENLY, I FELT AN INNER FEAR, AS YOU MAGICALLY DISAPPEARED

SOMEBODY WOKE ME UP ! ! !

THESE ARE WORDS THAT COME STRAIGHT FROM MY HEART

MY LOVE IS CONTAINED AND GRAMMATICALLY ARRANGED
INTO WORDS THAT COME STRAIGHT FROM MY HEART

THE CONSTRUCTION OF IDEAS PRESERVED
AND CONCEALED OUT OF SYMBOLS

'THANKS TO AN ANCIENT WRITTEN ART'

REMINISCENCE OF WHEN WE FIRST KISSED
INTIMACIES OF HOW MUCH YOU ARE MISSED
INSIDE AN ENVELOPE THAT SERVES AS AN ARK

FROZEN IN TIME UNTIL IT REACHES YOUR MIND
THROUGH CORRESPONDENCE THAT RIDES IN A CART

THE POWER OF INTERPRETATION RELEASES INFORMATION
COMPREHENSION THUS LEAVING ITS MARK

THE D-I-S-T-A-N-C-E MAY BE LONG, BUT
OUR COMMITMENT IS SO STRONG,
OUR COMMUNICATION WILL
NEVER BREAK APART

THIS IS MY WAY OF BRIGHTENING YOUR DAY
BY REAFFIRMING WHAT I SAID FROM THE START

THESE ARE WORDS THAT COME STRAIGHT FROM MY HEART

THANKS AGAIN

I FELT BETRAYAL'S DEEPEST PAIN MANY TIMES BEFORE

THE PAIN HAD STAINED MY PRECIOUS HEART
AND I COULD NOT FEEL LOVE ANYMORE

IT DISTORTED MY SENSE OF BELONGING
AND DAMAGED MY EMOTIONAL CORE

MY RELATIONSHIPS BECAME BATTLE
GROUNDS TO WIN OR TO LOSE AT WAR

*   *   *   *

WHEN YOU CAME INTO MY LIFE YOU
BROUGHT BACK LOVE'S REWARDS

MY LONELINESS HAS DISAPPEARED
MY HAPPINESS IS RESTORED

THANKS AGAIN FOR SHOWING ME
THAT LIFE IS WORTH LIVING FOR

WITH YOU I LEARNED TO LOVE AGAIN AND
HOW TO LOCK THOSE PAINFUL DOORS

SPIRITUALITY

SPIRITUAL EPIGRAM

THE INFINITE BEING CREATES, OUT OF WHICH INFINITE DEGREES OF CONSCIOUSNESS DECIDES ITS OWN FATE

IT'S THE ONLY WAY TO UNDERSTAND THE ORIGIN OF THE UNIVERSE -YOU MUST LOOK INWARD TO DISCOVER HOW YOUR DREAMS WORK

THOUGHT PROJECTION, A PULSATED HEART BEAT AND A RHYTHMIC DEEP BREATH ARE ALL CORRESPONDING MANIFESTATIONS OF LIFE AND DEATH.

LIFE BECOMES VERY SPECIAL WHEN WE DISCOVER THAT WE DID NOT COME HERE TO STAY.

IF THE REVELATION OF MY LIFE DOES NOT APPEAR AS A PRECIOUS LIFE SCENE TO AN ANGEL BEING THAN HOW COME IT KEEPS WATCHING OVER ME?

SOMEONE ONCE TOLD ME, "DEATH IS THE WORST EXPERIENCE IN LIFE." BUT I REPLIED,"THAT IS NOT NECESSARY SO, IF YOU HAVE NEVER PENETRATED THE WOMB OF CONSCIOUSNESS, HOW DO YOU KNOW WHERE YOURS WILL GO?"

STOP WORRYING ABOUT WHAT WILL HAPPEN TO YOU WHEN YOU DIE. YOU SHOULD BE WORRIED ABOUT WHAT WILL HAPPEN IF YOU LET YOUR PURPOSE IN LIFE PASS YOU BY.

WHEN WE MIX FAITH WITH ACTION WE WILL ALWAYS DO OUR BEST. GOD GUIDES THE FAITHFUL AND EFFORT TAKES CARE OF THE REST.

I HAVE NO REGRET, IF I SHOULD SUDDENLY DIE TODAY. FOR, WHAT I HAVE SEEN IN MY DEEPEST DREAMS, MOST PEOPLE MAY NEVER GET TO SEE FOR ALL ETERNITY.

THE CREATION STORY

BEFORE SPACE AND TIME OR WHEN THE UNIVERSE COULD BE SEEN
THERE WAS NOTHING IN EXISTENCE, BUT "THE INFINITE BEING"
AS IT IN-OUTWARDLY SEARCHED, FOR ITS OWN ORIGIN OF BIRTH
SELF - EXPRESSION EVOLVED INTO A POWERFUL BURST
MULTIDIMENSIONAL EXISTENCE, IT'S CREATIVITY DISPERSED
THE INFINITE ANIMATION – **A GOD/GODDESS   UNIVERSE**

WE ENTERED THE EARTH, THE WAY MINDS ENTER DREAMS
SIMULTANEOUSLY WE CREATE INSTANTANEOUS SCENES
THROUGH DIMENSIONS WE TRAVEL, IN EONS IT SEEMS

WE CHOOSE OUR OWN FORMS BETWEEN OPPOSITE BEINGS   **LIKE MAGIC**

FROM ATOMS TO WORLDS, WHERE COUNTLESS SPECIES UNFOLD
WE CAME FROM WITHIN, AND BACK WITHIN WE WILL GO
THE PURPOSE IN LIFE IS TO DEVELOP THE SPECIES SOULS
AND WHEN THE MISSION IS FULFILLED, OR THE PATTERN GROWS OLD
THERE'S THE CALLING OF DEATH, THE MOST INTENSE EPISODE

FOR HUMANITY, THERE'S A STOP, WHERE WE ALL WILL BE DROPPED
CLEANSING THE SPIRIT - WHILE THE FLESH LAYS TO ROT
COMPARING/REMINISCING; PAST, PRESENT, PROBABLE EXISTENCE
RESURRECTING FROM MENTAL STOCK, SOULS CREATING NEW PLOTS

TO THIS WORLD WE CAN RETURN, FOR NEW LESSONS TO LEARN
THIS LIFE IS JUST A TRAINING GROUND, FOR ALL SPECIES TO EARN
A JOURNEY TO INNER WORLDS, WHERE THERE ARE NO CONCERNS
JUST EVIDENCE OF WHAT, SACRED SCRIPTURES CONFIRM, THAT:

PARADISE IS CREATED OUT OF PURE RIGHTEOUSNESS
IT'S WHERE JUST SOULS INHERIT ROLES AS GODS AND GODDESSES
PRECIOUS MEMORIES INHERIT QUALITIES OF ETERNAL BLISS
AND EACH EXPERIENCE IS LIVED THROUGH PEACE AND HAPPINESS

THIS PLACE WE CALL UNIVERSE, IS ONLY JUST A DREAM
CONCEIVED IN THE MIND OF "THE INFINITE BEING"
THE PROOF TO THIS STORY IS PRESERVED IN YOUR GENES
JUST LOOK DEEP WITHIN AND IT WILL FLASH ON THE SCREEN
                          OF
                                  YOUR
                                            PSYCHE

THE ULTIMATE DREAM

WHAT IF THE UNIVERSE IS REALLY A DREAM, CONCEIVED IN THE MIND OF THE INFINITE BEING AS "THE ONLY MEANS BY WHICH IT COULD KNOW ITSELF"

WHAT IF THE ORIGIN OF THIS MIRACULOUS DREAM BROUGHT-FORTH THE DIVINE POWER OF CREATIVITY, BURSTING INTO EXISTENCE FOREVER, FORMING MULTIDIMENSIONAL PLANES WITH INFINITE DEGREES OF REALITIES, ALL AT ONCE.

WHAT IF WITHIN THIS ULTIMATE DREAM LIES THE BLUEPRINT OF ETERNITY, THE DOOR TO IMMORTALITY, THE HOME-BASE WHERE EVERYTHING SIMULTANEOUSLY MEETS, INTERACTS AND EXCHANGES PLACES, TRANSCENDING TIME IN THE SAME SPACE, PLANES EXISTING WITHIN PLANES, IN SPHERES THAT SEPARATE BY RATES THAT VIBRATES, BUT NEVER REST. WHAT IF THIS ULTIMATE DREAM MANIFESTS ITSELF AS, "AN ETERNAL COSMIC BREATH?"

WHAT IF THIS ULTIMATE DREAM WAS CREATED OUT OF THE INFINITE BEING'S OWN CONSTITUTION, FOREVER CONTAINED IN A FIXED STATE OF EVOLUTION, TRANSFORMING EVERGY INTO A POWERFUL PROJECTION, THUS COMMANDED BY THE WILL OF ITS OWN SELF-EXPRESSION; WHAT IF THIS EXPRESSION IS JUST ANOTHER NAME FOR "THE BIG BANG" OR THE GREAT POLAR SPLIT INTO TWO OPPOSITES, THE ANCIENTS CALLED GOD AND NATURE "THE GODDESS," AND IT WAS THESE GODS THAT CREATED ALL LIFE OUT OF THEIR SPIRITUAL CONSCIOUSNESS

WHAT IF EVERYTHING DECIDES ITS OWN FATE, BY CHOICES THAT ARE MADE IN THE DREAM STATE, NEUTRONS DREAMT OF PROTONS THAT STOOD STILL AND ELECTRONS THAT ROTATE; HENCE THE LIFE OF ALL MATTER INITIATES, OUT OF PLANETARY DREAMS ALL SPECIES SPRING INTO JOINT OR SEPARATE GENDER LOVE-BEINGS

WHAT IF THE HUMAN SPECIES IS A JOINT CLUSTERED ENTITY, COMPOSED OF COUNTLESS SOULS, EACH SOUL CREATING UNLIMITED PERSONALITIES; WHAT IF EACH PERSONALITY'S GOAL IS TO BECOME ITS OWN SOUL BY MANIFESTING GOD-GODDESS-LIKE ABILITIES, FROM FINITE INTO AN EXISTENCE OF INFINITY.

WHAT IF EVERYTHING IS REALLY JUST A DREAM. AND DREAMS DREAMT DREAMS OF OTHER DREAMS, BUT NONE CAN ESCAPE "THE ULTIMATE DREAM" CONCEIVED BY THE INFINITE BEING

THE GODS

WE ARE MULTI-DIMENSIONAL ENTITES, OUR EXISTENCE
LIES BETWEEN MASCULINE AND FEMININITY, WE FORM THE
PATTERNS FOR ALL IDENTITIES, INDIVIDUALLY AND COLLECTIVELY
WE SPRING FROM THAT INFINITE SOURCE OF SPIRITUAL CAPACITY

WE CAN APPEAR, DISAPPEAR OR REAPPEAR FOR ALL ETERNITY,
WE CAN EXIST IN ALL REALITIES – SIMULTANEOUSLY - WE ARE
CLUSTERS OF HIGHLY EVOLVED SOULS, COMPOSED OF THAT GOD STUFF

OUR SOULS ARE ALSO SPIRITUAL VEHICLES, INHERITED, WITH THE INIFINITE
BEING'S ABILITY TO MULTIPLE OR DIVIDE, TO REMAIN AS ONE OR TO
INTERTWINE WITH MANY. WE ASSIST IN MANIFESTING THE PROPERTIES
OF ALL MATTER AND IN THE CREATION OF YOUR DIMENSIONAL TRINITY

OUR PURPOSE IN LIFE IS TO EXPERIENCE. EXPERIENCE ENRICHES OUR
SOULS. THE GREATEST JOY FOR US IS TO KNOW, BUT TO DO
SO, WE MUST CONSTANTLY ENFOLD AND / OR UNFOLD. SO WE
CREATED SPACE AND TIME UPON WHICH TO TRAVEL

WE STORE INSIGHT INTO 'STARLIGHTS' TO SERVE
AS A TRAIL BLAZE FOR THE EMERGENCE OF ALL
CONSCIOUS LIFE IN YOU – WE INSTILLED THE POWER
TO BECOME GOD - LIKE, BUT IF YOU FAIL TO CREATE YOU
WILL DISAPPEAR THE WAY THE DAY DOES AT NIGHT

WE ARE THE DWELLERS OF THAT HEAVENLY PLACE, IT IS
LARGER THAN YOUR ENTIRE UNIVERSE, BUT IT TAKES UP NO SPACE
IT IS WHERE WE ALL BATHE IN OUR PUREST CONSCIOUS STATE

IN YOUR MYTHS, WE ARE ALL CAMOUFLAGED
WE USE RELIGIONS TO APPEAR AS OUR GODS
WE ARE VERY ANCIENT AND STILL VERY NEW

IMAGINATION IS ONE OF OUR PORTALS TOO
LEAVE GUIDANCE FOR ALL CONSCIOUS MORTALS
AND THE SECRET TO THIS PRECIOUS GOLDEN RULE:

EARTHLY LESSONS ARE THE TRIALS YOU MUST GO THROUGH
OUR ENTITIES ARE WHAT YOU WILL EVOLVE INTO
YOU ARE REALLY US AND WE ARE REALLY YOU

**WE ARE THE GODS
AND YOU ARE GODS TOO!**

LIFE AFTER DEATH

NOW THAT I CAN FLY,
I WILL TRAVEL THROUGH YOUR EYES,
I WILL JOURNEY DEEP INSIDE YOUR MILKY WAY

THE FIRST THING I WILL DO,
IS TO WATCH OVER AND COMFORT YOU,
BEFORE I LET MY PRECIOUS BODY MELT A WAY

THEN I WILL TAKE A RIDE TO THE PLACE WHERE LOVE RESIDES
TO STAND RIGHT BY YOUR SIDE, THROUGH THICK AND THIN
LIKE A GRAPE VINE I WILL BEND UNTIL OUR SOULS BEGIN TO BLEND
AND REMAIN YOUR CLOSEST FRIEND - UNTIL THE VERY END

I WILL REDUCE MY WEIGHT AND GLIDE, INSIDE ALL YOUR NUCLEOTIDES,
UNTIL I REACH THAT SPECIAL PLACE, "ON THE OTHER SIDE"

I WILL THANK YOUR SPIRITUAL GUIDE, FOR MAKING YOU MY BRIDE,
THEN WAIT MY FATE FOR JUDGMENT, UNTIL GOD ARRIVES, TO GOD
I WILL MAKE THIS PLEA, FOR ALL YOUR RIGHTEOUS DEEDS,
IN PRAYER, I WILL RECITE THIS SOULFUL CRY:

**PLEASE, BLESS OUR EARTHLY LIVES AND
CONNECT OUR ETERNAL TIES, THEN TURN HER
HURT TO JOY SO SHE CAN LIVE HER LIFE**

I WILL DISCOVER THE REASON WHY IT WAS TIME FOR ME TO DIE
THEN HELP YOU COMPLETE YOUR LIFE AS YOU DECIDE, BUT
REMEMBER TO ALWAYS STRIVE, TO KEEP OUR BOND ALIVE, SO WE
CAN MEET AGAIN AS SOUL-MATES, "IN ANOTHER PLACE AND TIME"

I AM ALWAYS BY YOUR SIDE, SO WIPE YOUR TEARFUL EYES AND
FOLLOW THIS GOLDEN RULE, IT WILL CONNECT OUR LIVES:

**WE ARE SENT HERE TO BE TAUGHT HOW TO CREATE
REALITY OUT OF THOUGHTS AND HOW TO TRAVEL
BACK AND FORTH THROUGH PORTALS WITH OUR MINDS**

**YOUR IMAGINATION IS THE KEY TO KEEPING IN TOUCH WITH
ME, YOU CAN CALL ME IN YOUR DREAMS, 'AT ANY TIME'**

THAT PLACE WE ALL CALL HEAVEN IS WHERE I RESIDE

MY VERSION OF FRAMEWORK 1 & 2

I BELIEVE IN A PRIMARY CREATOR. ALL THINGS IN EXISTENCE ARE EVIDENCE OF ITS DIVINE NATURE. THIS SELF-CREATED PRIMARY SOURCE SPOUTS FORTH UNLIMITED CREATIVE CAPACITY OUT OF WHICH THE PHYSICAL UNIVERSE EMERGES.

I AM TOTALLY CONVINCED THAT MY IMAGINATION IS A PORTAL. IT TAKES ME INTO THOSE INNER REALMS OF ACTUALITY WHERE MY GOD-CENTERED SOURCE IS IMMORTAL. IT IS MY SOUL'S SPIRITUAL EYE, LOOKING OUTWARD INTO PHYSICAL REALITY AND USING THE POWER OF PROJECTION TO KEEP MY BODY ALIVE. MY IMAGINATION REFLECTS LIKE A REVERSIBLE PSYCHIC SCREEN. FROM WITHIN FLOWS OUTWARDLY AN AWARENESS, FREE WILL AND ENERGY THAT CONSTANTLY GENERATES MY PHYSICAL BEING. FROM OUTWARDLY FLOWS WITHIN MY EARTHLY EXPERIENCES I FEED TO MY SOUL IN THE FORM OF DREAMS.

MY BELIEF IN THESE CONCEPTS EXPANDS MY IMAGINATION AND ALLOWS FOR A PENDULUM FLOW OF THAT UNLIMITED CREATIVE CAPACITY. IT ALSO KEEPS ME IN TUNE WITH MY INNER SELF. I WILL PAY MORE ATTENTION TO THIS INNER VOICE AS IT SPEAKS TO ME THROUGH MY DREAMS, INPULSES, INNER VISION, DESIRES, EMOTIONS, FEELINGS AND THE EXTERNAL ENVIRONMENT.

ANYTHING I WANT IN THIS WORLD WILL COME TO ME FROM THAT VAST INTERNAL EXISTENCE: A PRODUCTIVE AND SUCESSFUL LIFE, EXCELLENT HEALTH AND LONGEVITY FOR ME, MY LOVED-ONES AND THE RIGHTEOUS DROVES OF HUMANITY. I AM NOT CONCERNED WITH PARTICULARS. I WILL SIMPLY RECITE THEM, THE INNER POWER OF CREATIVITY WILL MANIFEST THEM AND MY INNER SELF WILL DELIVER THEM FOR ME. IN APPRECIATION, I WILL HONOR THESE BLESSINGS WITH INTEGRITY.

THE DAILY RECITATION OF THIS CREED WILL INOCULATE MY MIND WITH COMPLETE CONFIDENCE IN THE WORKING RELATIONSHIP BETWEEN MY INNER AND OUTER SELF, THE ACHIEVEMENT OF MY GOALS, AND THE ULTIMATE EXPERIENCE OF VALUE FULFILLMENT.

THE ATHEIST

WHAT IF THE TRUTH WAS ON MY SIDE, SAID AN ATHEIST,
WHO CLAIMS THAT DEATH IS AN ETERNAL STATE OF NOTHINGNESS.
THEN THERE WOULD BE NO NEED FOR GOD TO BE WORSHIPPED,
NO DEVIL WOULD EXIST, NO RELIGIOUS WARS OR CONFLICTS,
ONLY EARTHLY EXISTENCE WOULD BE CONSIDERED AS PRICELESS

WHAT IF DEATH WAS AN ETERNAL STATE OF NOTHINGNESS, A LIFE
SPAN OF A MILLION YEARS WOULD BE CONSIDERED TOO SHORT, THERE
WOULD BE NO TIME WASTING, SUICIDES, OR FETUS TO ABORT,
WARS WOULD HAVE NEVER BEEN FOUGHT, OR HATRED EVER TAUGHT,
MURDER WOULD BE LOOKED UPON AS THE MOST SENSELESS

ENJOYING LIFE WOULD BECOME THE ONLY REAL PURPOSE

EVEN SEX WOULD BE UPHELD AS PURELY SACRED
MORE THAN LUST WOULD BE FELT IN A KISS
LIFE'S ACTIONS WOULD CONSIST OF A HEAVENLY BLISS
EACH MOMENT WOULD BE APPROACHED AS PURE HAPPINESS
FOR NO JOY COULD REPLACE THAT ULTIMATE STATE OF

'NOTHINGNESS'

WHAT IF NOTHINGNESS WAS THE STATE OF LIFE'S FINAL FATE
ALL MEMORIES WOULD BE ERASED, LEAVING NOTHING TO TRACE
BUT FEAR IN OUR HEARTS WITH EACH BREATH THAT WE TAKE
EACH MOMENT WE ARE REMINDED OF AN EXPIRATION DATE
WHEN OUR LIVES ARE CONSUMED INTO THAT EMPTY STATE OF

'NOTHINGNESS'

THEN JUST MAYBE,

AS A SPECIES WE WOULD ALL STRIVE TO APPREICATE OUR LIVES
BECAUSE EVERYONE WOULD BE TOO AFRAID TO DIE
OR EVAPATE INTO THAT EMPTY STATE OF NOTHINGNESS !

" SO SAID THE ATHEIST "

AND THE THEOLOGIAN RESPONDED

MY DEAR ATHEIST FRIEND:

THE REAL PURPOSE IN THIS LIFE YOU HAVE CLEARLY MISSED
FOR, EVERYTHING YOU SEE APPEARS BECAUSE GOD EXIST
AND **"THE GREAT MYSTERY OF DEATH"** IS JUST PART OF IT

YOUR ARGUMENT ABOUT DEATH IS ONE OF THE OLDEST HUMAN DEBATES
BE WARE! FOR, WHAT YOU BELIEVE CAN BECOME A MANIFESTATION OF FATE
THAT IS WHY WE BELIEVE IN A GOD WHO WILL DELIVER US THROUGH FAITH

IN OUR DEEPEST CONVICTION WE HOLD THIS FAITH TO BE DEAR
AS FOR DEATH WE RELINQUISH, TO GOD, ALL OF OUR FEARS!

I KNOW TO YOU ALL OF THIS MAY SEEM SO VERY ODD
THAT SO MANY PEOPLE WOULD PLACE ALL OF THEIR FAITH IN A GOD?

*   *   *   *

BEFORE YOU DISMISS MY OPINION

STUDY THE UNDERLYING PRINCIPLES BEHIND ALL RELIGIONS
AND YOU TOO WILL AGREE, THEY ARE SACRED AND DIVINE

STUDY THE LAWS OF NATURE AND YOU TOO WILL SEE
THAT EVERYTHING IS INTELLIGENTLY DESIGNED

THEN CONSIDER THIS:

THE POLARITY OF GOOD AND EVIL WILL ALWAYS EXIST
THE HUMAN MIND DEVELOPS ITSELF THROUGH OPPOSITES
TO SET CHALLENGES, TO ADDRESS OUR OWN INNER CONFLICTS
SO THAT LIFE LESSONS CAN BUILD CHARACTER AND RIGHTEOUSNESS

AND YES, AS A SPECIES, WE CAN STRIVE TO APPREICATE OUR LIVES
EVEN THROUGH, IN THE FINAL ANALYSIS, WE ALL MUST STILL DIE
IT'S JUST THAT WE BELIEVE THERE IS A BETTER PLACE WHERE SOULS RESIDE
BUT THE CHOICE TO LIVE IN PEACE OR CONFLICT IS STILL YOUR AND MINE

*   *   *   *

SURE, THERE ARE THOSE WHO HAVE KILLED IN THE NAME OF GOD'S RELIGIONS
BUT I WILL CONTINUE TO STRIVE TO BE A TRUE BELIEVER WITH ONE AMIBITION
TO LIVE BY THE DOCTRINE OF CHRIST AND SERVE AS A RIGHTEOUS CHRISTIAN
IN PARADISE, I WILL SEEK MY REWARDS, AS I MAKE MY HEAVENLY TRANSITION
AS FOR THOSE WHO CONTINUE TO ABUSE, I WILL PRAY FOR THEM AND FOR YOU,

"OH LORD! PLEASE, TOUCH THEIR HEARTS:
AND MAKE MY MISSION THEIR MISSION TOO"

BE WISE MY DEAR FRIEND:

IF YOU ARE RIGHT AND I AM WRONG THEN DEATH OFFERS US BOTH NOTHING
BUT IF, YOU ARE WRONG AND I AM RIGHT, I AM GUARANTEED SOMETHING,

"A SPECIAL PLACE IN GOD'S PARADISE"

*   *   *   *

NOTE:

IMMOTALITY IS A COMMON BELIEF AMOUNGST MOST WOMEN AND MEN
BUT GOD IS FORGIVING, AND TO THE IGNORANCE, HE MAKES AMEND
NO ONE SHALL BE PUNISHED FOR WHAT THEY CHOOSE TO BELIEVE IN
SO AS LONG AS THEY CHOOSE TO LIVE RIGHTEOUSLY OVER SIN

LIVE IN RIGHTEOUSNESS MY FRIEND
AND GOD WILL DELIVER YOU FROM SIN

"SO SAID THE THEOLOGIAN"

ATONEMENT

ATONEMENT BEGINS WITH THE DEBT OWED
BUT NEVER ENDS - EVEN AFTER THE DEBT IS PAID

ATONEMENT IS TO ACCEPT THE RESPONSIBILITY TO
AMEND – TO DO AWAY WITH ALL ACTS THAT OFFEND

TO RESTORE OURSELVES TO RIGHTEOUS WOMEN OR MEN
TO GIVE BACK, IN GOOD DEEDS, WHENEVER WE CAN

ATONEMENT IS THE MEASUREMENT FOR WHICH WE ALL WILL
BE TESTED, THE PROCESS BY WHICH WE WILL BE ACCEPTED

THE CONTRACT TO A LIFETIME COMMITMENT
A COMING TOGETHER FOR A RIGHTEOUS UPLIFTMENT

IDEA PROJECTION

WHEN IDEAS ARE FIRST CONCEIVED
THEY CREATE THEIR OWN PROJECTION

THROUGH PERSONAL EXPERIENCE AND JOINT
EVENTS THEY MANIFEST THEIR OWN EXPRESSION

MEMORIES, PATTERNS AND IDENTITIES
ARE HOW THEY LEAVE IMPRESSIONS

*   *   *   *

WHEN CALLING UPON THE PAST THEY
RE-APPEAR AS VALUABLE LESSONS

THROUGH DIFFICULT TIMES THEY GUIDE
US AND PROVIDES US WITH PROTECTION

IDEAS ARE DESIGNED TO FULFILL OUR
LIVES WITH EARTHLY BLESSINGS

INNOCENCE

FOR BEING INNOCENT AND POOR, A
LIFE SENTENCE CONCEALED MY FATE, TO
MAINTAIN MY COMMITMENT TO EXONERATE,
I MUST RELY UPON STRENGTH AND INNER FAITH

RECANTATION, CORRUPTION AND NEW EVIDENCE
WAS NEVER KNOWN TO MY TRIAL JURY, AFTER
34-PLUS L-O-N-G YEARS OF DENIALS. STILL,
NO ONE WILL BELIEVE MY STORY!

EXCERPTS FROM MY MEMOIR:

"Imagine having lived the first 17 years of your life in a social context. Then suddenly you are kidnapped and held captive in a cage for over 3 decades for something you had absolutely nothing to do with. Imagine turning 50 years of age and never having had the opportunity to live your life as an 'adult,' free of incarceration . . . Imagine being forced to perceive from inside of a cage the society you now live in as 'the outside world.' Then try to imagine living with the prospect of freedom as your ultimate desire, or dying in prison as your ultimate fear. Knowing you may never again experience a normal life in the outside world with the people you love the most. To imagine this would give you an idea of who I am and why I must tell you this story . . .

"Giving up my innocence would be like foolishly giving up my passport into heaven or like my soul unjustifiably surrendering my personality to the kind of death equivalent to an eternal state of nothingness, a place where minds are confined to perceptions with no outward expressions. To voluntarily submit to a senseless murder I would never commit would strip me of all my worth and contradict my existence on this earth and the hereafter . . ."

*   *   *   *   *

"In June 1976, I was sent to Elmira Reception Center (NYS) for testing and orientation . . . When we approached the locking locations I was caught by total surprise. While we waited for the officer to unlock the entrance gate, I peeked into the interior. I never witnessed a locking location consisting of so many people in one area. The distance between the first and last cell seemed a mile long, with four layers of tiers on both sides. Prisoners were going crazy as we entered into what felt like an ancient monolithic gladiator school. The noise level reminded me of that of a college football game . . ."

"To compound the situation, one of the prisoners who arrived with me had long blond hair down his back. As we made our way to our cells all we could hear were loud rhythmic shouts of, 'new-jacks, new-jacks, new-jacks!' Eventually the shouts quickly switched to 'blondie, blondie!' Simultaneously, paper bags and other burning materials were thrown from all levels of the tiers. As we continued to walk to our respective cells, I could also hear some prisoners yelling: 'You pretty mother fucker, I want to fuck you!' The noise level continued for almost five minutes after we locked in. Then it slowly subsided. I would later discover that this kind of introduction was a common practice that had somehow been cemented into an Elmira tradition. That tradition was Elmira's warm way of saying, 'welcome to hell'. . !"

"The Box" (special housing unit 'SHU' as it is now called) had its own uniqueness. The strong element of despair created its aura, leaving the night hours dense with a hollow, lonely-like emptiness. It had a way of dictating one's moods, feelings and emotions; as well as the ability to manipulate a weak mind into submission. These conditions intensified as the number of those confined decreased or when all verbal communication ceased. In addition to its psychological affects, the harsh mistreatment by guards triggered my inner gut feeling of déjà vu, my own genetic connection of an updated version of modern slavery . . ."

"During quietness, the past had a way of transcending the boundaries of space and time. Re-emerging through a writing legacy that filled the cell walls. One could read the foolish pride and dying thirst for recognition even at the expense of one's own suffering: 'Big Mike was here and now he is gone, he left his name to carry on.' There were simple messages of loneliness written on the ceiling directly above my head, one of which read: 'Debbie I love you.' But the phrase that struck me the most was a reference to jail as . . .'this man made hell.' It jumped out at me like a swift spark of illumination. It seemed so relative to a description of truth that even today I still consider imprisonment as such. At first, I wanted to write my own legacy but then I thought, only fools seek glory in <u>Hell</u> . . ."

*   *   *   *   *

"I had been in prison for 9 years and was, for the first time, coming to the realization of what my tribulations were creating in me. Like many prisoners, I had been introduced to valuable information but was not developing. What I considered development was purely superficial. The only thing I was doing was pouring information on top of the deep internal conflicts I had never bothered to acknowledge, let alone addressed. I accepted it as a natural part of what I was experiencing. At that time in my life, I had no real understanding of the true meaning of development . . ."

"In spite of the negative impact my prison experience was having on me, it was not the sum total of my existence. I was always able to draw from the core of my inner strength. It gave me hope and courage. In addition, I drew from the strength of my family and the knowledge that I had many people from my community on my side. In my mind I painted this picture and lived with the vision and belief that someday I would be free. Even when my days were dim, my future seemed uncertain, my inner strength would always guide me back to this state of rationality and inner peace. This inner source of capacity served as my demigod . . ."

*   *   *   *   *

"The prison experience shattered my reality and redefined my view of the world. At times loneliness, hurt and anger became my greatest enemies. They fought against my sanity/demigod for possession of my wounded spirit. Living the life of a slave in a prison cage clouded my sensitivity and gave birth to negativity's twin forces of hatred and revenge. Looking back was nothing more than a reminder of how the best years of my life had been washed away in the rainstorm of injustice. Part of my human potential got trapped in the passing of time . . ."

"At times it felt like the cumulative negative forces had invaded a virgin territory and formed their own region. I know this was the result of internalizing so much pain. Consequently, it reigned supreme in my subconscious. It came to me in the form of mental stress and loneliness. They were the warning signs that this experience was slowing destroying me on the inside. These signs indicated to me that it was time for me to develop a cure that involved some form of internal transformation. The more I learned the more apparent it became. I had to take my internal pilgrimage. The guidance of my ancestors, the blessings of my elders, nor the wisdom of my family and freinds could take me there. The requisite journey to self-empowerment was my responsibility, and mine alone . . ."

IF YOU CAN ANSWER THIS ONE, THEN TELL ME,

WHY MUST THE GOOD DIE YOUNG?

THROUGH THE BLESSINGS OF GOD – LIFE SUDDENLY APPEARS
IT'S THE BIRTH OF A CHILD – JUBILEE FILLS THE AIR
THERE ARE KISSES AND HUGS – AND WARM JOYFUL TEARS
FOR A LIFE THAT WOULD LAST – ONLY FOR VERY SHORT YEARS

IF YOU CAN ANSWER THIS ONE, THEN TELL ME,
WHY MUST THE GOOD DIE YOUNG?

IT WAS TWO-DAYS AFTER A PARTY – A FRIEND WAS FOUND DECEASED
MANY PEOPLE WOULD SUFFER – A COMMUNITY SHOCKED IN DISBELIEF
WHO WOULD DO SUCH A THING – COMMITTING THIS TERRIBLE SIN
IT WAS A SAD WAY TO END – AN ACT THAT CRIED OUT REVENGE!

IF YOU CAN ANSWER THIS ONE, THEN TELL ME,
WHY MUST THE GOOD DIE YOUNG?

OH, AT THE BURIAL SITE – WHILE STANDING IN FEAR
MINDS CONFUSED – HEARTS DROWNING IN TEARS
FOR THE DEATH OF A LOVED ONE – WHO WILL NOW DISAPPEAR
AS YOU PIERCE THROUGH SPACE – IN AN OUTWARD FIXED STARE

- WONDERING -

WHERE DO WE COME FROM?   *   WHERE WILL WE GO FROM HERE?

IF YOU CAN ANSWER THIS ONE, THEN TELL ME,
WHY MUST THE GOOD DIE YOUNG?

FALSELY ACCUSED WITH BLAME – YOUTH VIOLENTLY SEIZED IN VAIN
MANIPULATED AND FRAMED – HELD THIRTY-TWO-PLUS YEARS IN CHAINS
SUFFERING CONSUMING MY BRAIN – DENIALS ARE LEAVING ME DRAINED
GRIEF, HURT, SORROW AND PAIN – TRYING TO DRIVE ME INSANE
LOVE IN MY HEART HAS BEEN STRAINED – BUT YET, MY QUESTIONS REMAINS

IF YOU CAN ANSWER THIS ONE,

PLEASE THEN TELL ME,

WHY MUST THE GOOD DIE YOUNG?

DESECRATING THE HOLY BIBLE:
IN THE NAME OF GOD

Over 200 years ago, the United States Supreme Court concluded that: "No person in the United States . . . can put himself above the basic law of the constitution. That is why Americans can say, ours is a government of laws, not of men" (Marbury v. Madison), 1 Cranch 137, 163 (1803)). Of all the rights provided for in the Constitution, the right to the freedom of religion is the most sacred and is guaranteed to all Americans, including those who suffer incarceration. "Judgment Day," when it will be determined by the Creator who will reside in the hereafter, (a belief commonly shared by all major religions of the world), comes to pass only upon death. The high court, over 50 years ago, in solidification of the right to believe in a particular religious faith, also concluded that: "Men may believe what they can not prove" (United States v. Ballard, 64 S. Ct. 882 (19__)).

Religion was deemed to be of such significance that it was cemented into the foundation of our institutions. "IN GOD WE TRUST" is prominently displayed in our halls of justice, and is imprinted on the currency that we utilized in conducting the nation's commerce. The trial testimonial oath is administered in God's name, Early American patriots surely recognized the sacredness and importance of God, or they would not have made it s prerequisite in giving trial testimony to invoke God's name while using the Holy Bible to transform the oath into a solemn, holy pledge. Religiously-bound testimony in a court of law makes the testifier not only subject to the laws of perjury in the secular world, but also makes him/her accountable to God on the Day of Judgment in the hereinafter.

In the Christian faith, the authenticity of the Ten Commandments are branded in the hearts of true believers. Thus, a true believer's faith cannot be subverted by requiring him or her to disavow a solemn, religiously-taken oath, enjoined on them by law for the sake of administrative expediency. One of the Ten Commandments emphatically states: "Thou shalt not take the name of the Lord thy God in vain, for the Lord will not hold him guiltless that taketh his name in vain." (Exodus 20:7). No court can claim to protect the right to religion if that court will not protect a person against retaliation for exercising the right to adhere to a sacred oath taken in the name of God.

Current Supreme Court decisions have allowed the diminishment of rights of the incarcerated when those rights are outweighed by legitimate penological objectives. However, the right to freedom of religion, while not immune from diminishment, enjoys far greater consideration than other constitutionally-guaranteed rights. The Religious Land Use and Institutionalized Person Act protects the right to freedom of religion to individuals under the care, custody, and control of, inter alia, a penal institution. Even foreign enemy combatants, insurgents, and terrorists held in American custody are able to engage in religious practices.

When allegations first surfaced concerning the desecration of the Holy Quran, the Islamic religious text, top United States government officials called for an investigation into the matter, and promised that appropriate actions would be taken if the allegations proved true. A small group of Americans of different religious persuasions went so far as to buy copies of the Holy Quran in an interfaith display of religious solidarity. But little does this group and other Americans know, two departments in the criminal justice system engage in regular desecration of the Holy Bible, and have placed themselves above God.

In the State of New York, prisoners are routinely required to admit their guilt to the crimes they have been convicted of if they are to entertain the slightest hope of securing their freedom on parole. Such admissions of guilt are demanded notwithstanding the fact that some of these prisoners are in fact not guilty and took an oath in God's name before the Holy Bible. For State administrative agencies to render meaningless prisoners' right to adhere to and practice the dictates and precepts of their religious faith, for the sole purpose of administrative expedience, is tantamount to and just as reprehensible as flushing the Holy Bible down a toilet. American democracy, as set forth in both Federal and New York State Constitutions, provides for the right of American citizens to choose to pursue or adhere to a religious faith. If a State agency chooses not to believe in God or the Holy Bible, then that is their constitutionally-protected prerogative, but our sense of democracy does not entitle agencies to impose their lack of faith upon those under their charge. To the contrary, those agencies are enjoined from discriminating against a person's practice of his or her religious faith.

In 1975, I was charged with a murder I did not commit. In 1976, prior to testifying at trial in my own defense, I stood before the Holy Bible and raised my right hand, and swore to tell the truth. I then testified in open court and professed, in the name of God and in accord with my faith in Christianity, my complete innocence to the crimes upon which I was being tried. Even though I was found guilty by a jury who relied solely upon the prosecution's star witness, (who has since recanted her testimony), I never wavered on my claim of innocence, nor have I forsaken the oath I took in God's name on the Holy Bible.

As a consequence for the longstanding choice to adhere to the oath I took in God's name my minimum sentence of 20 years had been extended 12 years, the imposition of six 2-year holds. My innocence and religious conviction prevents me from ever betraying the testimonial oath I took at trial. As a consequence, I was made to suffer dearly for refusing to give up both my personal principles and precious Constitutional right to religious freedom.

Furthermore, testifying under oath is so powerful that many people including athletes and entertainers have been haunted, tried and some convicted/sentenced to prison for allegedly committing perjury under oath. These are the same courts that routinely reject the recantation of a prosecution's key witness who comes forward and admits to lying under oath for having convicted a person in a criminal trial. Although committing perjury under oath is a crime, prisoners who testified to being innocence under oath, are required to violate that oath and admit guilt as a prerequisite for parole release consideration? Of course, no laws are written to prevent prosecutors from charging this same prisoner with perjury for testifying to being innocent at trial and then admit to guilt in exchange for a possible release. It is as ridiculous as the courts now relying on DNA evidence to convict but rejecting this same evidence when it clearly points to exclusion of a person wrongly convicted as is the current predicament of my plight. These are the kinds of inconsistencies that leave America's criminal justice system drowning in its own contradictions.

Who then will answer these very pertinent questions: Does the trial testimonial oath have religious implications? If so, does the Equal Protection Clause of the Fourteenth Amendment protect against retaliation for adhering to the oath? If religious implications are not involved in the oath in question, why are courts of our judiciary, offending citizen's religious beliefs by meaninglessly invoking God and using the Holy Bible as a prerequisite to the giving of trial testimony?

THE TRIAL OATH

WHO WROTE THE TESTIMONIAL TRIAL OATH?

ITS WORDS OF IMPORT,
SO SACRED IN VALUE,
SO SIMPLE TO QUOTE:

**"DO YOU SWEAR TO TELL THE TRUTH, THE WHOLE TRUTH
AND NOTHING BUT THE TRUTH, SO HELP YOU GOD?"**

THE OATH I GAVE WAS MADE SACRED AND RELIGIOUSLY BOUND BY
INVOCATION, USING GOD'S NAME TO TRANSFORM TESTIMONY INTO A
SOLEMN HOLY PLEDGE, AS I, STILL BEFORE THE HOLY BIBLE,
I RAISED MY RIGHT HAND AND SAID:

I DO!

PLEDGING BEFORE THE HOLY BIBLE IN GOD'S NAME, MAKES
US ACCOUNTABLE TO GOD'S CLAIM. AGAIN I QUOTE:

**"THOU SHALT NOT TAKE THE NAME OF THE LORD THY
GOD IN VAIN; FOR THE LORD WILL NOT HOLD HIM
GUILTLESS THAT TAKETH HIS NAME IN VAIN."**

EXODUS 20:7

THE COURT TURNED MY TRIAL TESTIMONY INTO A RELIGIOUS CONFESSION
THEN STRIPPED ME OF MY FIRST AMENDMENT PROTECTION

I HAVE SERVED 12 ADDITIONAL YEARS IN A
PRISON CAGE FOR A CRIME I DID NOT COMMIT

ONLY TO BE TOLD THE SACREDNESS OF WHAT
I TESTIFIED TO AT TRIAL DON'T MEAN SHIT

THEIR VERSION OF JUSTICE DEMANDS:

EVEN THOUGH YOU ARE INNOCENT,
TO GUILT YOU MUST NOW SUBMIT

BUT WHAT ABOUT THE SACREDNESS OF TESTIMONY GIVEN IN THE NAME OF GOD?

ITS MEANING DENOTES, LET US MAKE SACRED THIS POWERFUL OATH
BUT IN PRACTICE THERE ARE THOSE ABUSING AND TREATING IT AS A JOKE!
CREATING A CHRISTIAN FACADE, DISRESPECTING THE BIBLE AND GOD

BEWARE! SOME OF THEM ARE, ATHEISTLY CAMOUFLAGED IN JUSTICE GARBS
CONSTANTLY IN SEARCH OF INNOCENT SOULS TO ROB
AS THEY SIT ON THRONES PLAYING PSEUDO EARTH-GODS!

BY REQUIRING BUT NOT RESPECTING THE OATH'S SACREDNESS,
IN THE COURT OF LAW THE JUDICIARY WILL BE
CONSIDERATING GOD AND THE BIBLE MEANINGLESS

TO UNDERMINE AND OFFEND WHAT WE BELIEVE TO BE SO VERY DEAR
IS LIKE SOMEONE ATTACKING GOD WHILE WE STAND THERE IN FEAR

THE RELIGIOUS QUESTION:

DO I HAVE THE RIGHT TO UPHOLD AS SACRED MY
TESTIMONIAL TRIAL OATH, FOR HAVING GIVEN IT
BEFORE THE HOLY BIBLE AND IN THE NAME OF GOD ?

THEN I END WITH THIS NOTE:

**"PLEAD MY CAUSE, O LORD, WITH THEM THAT
STRIVE WITH ME: FIGHT AGAINST
THEM THAT FIGHT AGAINST ME."**

PSALM 35.1

THE LAST QUESTION:

IF GOD IS FIRST IN
YOUR LIFE, THEN
THIS IS ALSO
YOUR FIGHT

INHUMANE CONTRADICTIONS

HOW CAN YOU FORGIVE YOUR FOUNDING FATHERS FOR
THE ENSLAVEMENT AND VICIOUS SLAUGHTER OF MILLIONS
OF NATIVE AMERICANS AND AFRICAN SONS AND DAUGHTERS?

HOW CAN YOU FORGIVE AMERICAN SOLDIERS FOR KILLING
INNOCENT PEOPLE IN PROFIT-DRIVEN WARS WHILE YOU OVERLOOK
YOUR SOCIAL PRACTICE OF DISCRIMINATION AGAINST THE POOR?

HOW CAN YOU FORGIVE YOUR THUG-POLICE FOR CORRUPTION, COERCION,
TERRORISM AND EVEN MURDER, OR YOUR COURTS FOR SLOWLY SHUTTING
THE OPPORTUNITY DOOR; ELIMINATING THE HUMAN RIGHTS THE POOR
HAVE SINCERE FOUGHT FOR , SOME OF WHOM HAVE EVEN DIED FOR?

BUT !

YOU WILL NOT FORGIVE THE INCARCERATED; THAT IS, **THOSE WHO
WANT TO MAKE AMENDS;** YOU CONTINUE TO PUNISH EVEN
HARSHER THE WRONGFULLY CONVICTED JUST BECAUSE
WE   MAINTAIN   THAT   WE   DID   NOT   OFFEND

IF YOU CONTINUE TO PRACTICE THE LEGACY OF
THESE HISTORICAL TRENDS, YOU MUST REMEMBER
THAT GOD WILL BLESS NO COUNTRY WHO
PRACTICES INHUMANE CONTRADICTIONS

THE CRIMINAL INJUSTICE SYSTEM

THIRTY-TWO-PLUS YEARS OF FALSE IMPRISONMENT HAVE PIERCED
MY SOUL. CONSISTENT DENIALS TURNED ME FROM YOUNG TO OLD
AND YOU WONDER, WHY? WHY DOES HE ACT SO COLD ? COULD
IT BE BECAUSE MY EXPERIENCE HAS TAUGHT ME,
NOTHING HAS CHANGED ! THE PLANTATION AND
PRISON SYSTEM ARE ONE AND THE SAME

FUCK YOUR CRIMINAL INJUSTICE SYSTEM !

AND ALL YOU FAKE-ASS PATRIOTS, PRETENDING
TO REPRESENT JUSTICE IN THE NAME OF
DEMOCRACY, OR SHOULD I SAY, IN
THIS STOLEN LAND WHERE ONLY THE
RICH AND LIKED RECEIVE EQUALITY

SIT YOUR ASS DOWN MRS. LIBERTY

I AM SICK AND TIRED OF YOUR FUCKIN' HYPOCRISY
STANDING FOR JUSTICE IN DISGUISE
PRETENDING TO LOVE US ALL
ARE NOTHING BUT LIES

I KNOW YOU CAN SEE, SO TAKE THAT TRANSPARENT
CLOTH FROM AROUND YOUR EYES

HOW IN THE HELL CAN YOU BE BLIND:

WHEN IT COMES TO OPPRESSION AND INCARCERATION
THE POOR ARE THE ONLY ONES YOU CAN FIND

WHEN IT COMES TO CREATING AND ENFORCING LAWS
YOU DO SO TO PROTECT YOUR OWN WEALTHY KIND

AND YOU REALLY EXPECT ME TO
BELIEVE NONE OF THIS IS BY DESIGN

*   *   *   *   *

THAT'S RIGHT !   YOU HEARD WHAT I SAID:

FUCK YOUR CRIMINAL INJUSTICE SYSTEM !

AND IF YOU DON'T LIKE THIS POEM THEN,

FUCK YOU TOO ! ! !

CULTURAL RESURRECTION

A CULTURAL RESURRECTION

OH, GREAT RIVER NILE, YOUR
MIGHTY FLOW AMOUNTS TO
NOTHING WHEN COMPARED TO

THE CUMULATIVE AMOUNT OF
TEARS THAT FLOW OUT OF THE
AFRICAN HOLOCAUST SUFFERING

FREEDOM IS THE ULTIMATE GOAL! FOR THOSE WHO DEEPLY, DEEPLY
WANT IT, ONLY EFFORT WILL TAKE YOU DOWN THAT ROAD. TIME WILL NOT
WAIT FOR YOU, JUST LIKE TIME DID NOT WAIT FOR ME. THUS YOU MUST
PERSIST, PERSIST AND PERSIST, UNTIL YOU SUCCEED.

THE TOTAL LIBERATION AND DEVELOPMENT OF MY
MIND HAS BECOME MY ULTIMATE SIGHT OF DESTINY

WHO ARE YOU ?

I AM THE EVER-EVOLVING SUM TOTAL OF EVERYTHING
I HAVE EVER EXPERIENCED IN THIS LIFE

IN ESSENCE, I AM " IDEA CONSTRUCTION " EXCESSIVELY
CLOTHED IN THE DIVINE QUALITY OF MASCULINITY

OUT OF THE MANY MILLION POTENTIAL SPERM SPARKS OF LIFE
I AM THE ONE THAT SUCCEEDED IN THE BATTLE AND SPRUNG FORTH

- THE INNER NATURE OF MY EXISTENCE -

IN TRIPLE DARKNESS, I WAS CONCEIVED IN THE WOMB OF THE GODDESS MAAT
MY PHYSICAL COMPOSITION IS JUST AN IDEA OF MYSELF UNDER THE PROPERTY
OF MATTER, IT IS ONLY A VEHICLE THAT ENABLES ME TO LOOK OUTWARD

- TO VIEW YOUR PHYSICAL REALITY -

I WAS THE FIRST IN EXISTENCE, WHEN THE EARTH WAS STILL NEW
I MADE LOVE TO YOUR MOTHER "THE ANCIENT MISTRESS TIAMAT"
AND THEN I MADE YOU; BUT, I KNEW YOU WOULD BE LONELY SO I MADE

"THE BLACK WOMAN TOO"

IN ETHIOPIA, I TOOK SOOT FROM 'THE NILE' AND FASHIONED
DANKANESH ON MY POTTER WHEEL – I AM THE GOD KHNEMU !

I TRACE MY LINEAGE TO KHUWILAND – LAND OF THE GODS AND GODDESSES
BIRTHPLACE OF THE BLACK RACE, HOME OF BA-TUSA, BA-HUTI & BA-TWA
IN THE LAND OF AMEN-RA, THE POWERFUL, POWERFUL SUN-GOD

I AM THE RESURRECTION OF PAST MARTYRS, I AM YOUR LAST HOPE
SENT BY YOUR FOREMOTHERS & FATHERS, I COME TO RESURRECT THE YOUNG
AND THIS TIME I WON'T DIE TRYING, BECAUSE, I AM THE VICTORIOUS ONE !!!

WHAT MUST BE DONE TO
EMPOWER OUR CHILDREN

In spite of the current global crisis threatening the international economy, numbing national budgets and debilitating already struggling communities, we are forever confronted with the need to address this basic question: "What must be done to empower our children?"

Writer and poet Haki Madhubuti warns us, "A people's offspring are a priority. When people fail to place the development of its children as foremost on its list of priorities, that people is killing itself internally." As rational beings, we are equipped with a spiritual and innate genetic bond to nurture and develop our off springs. But whenever we fail to do so we undermine the very existence of our survival as a species.

There are many approaches we can pursue to empower our children in these troubling times. Empowerment begins at the pregnancy stage, where the overall health of a child is formed in the womb. A mother's spiritual, mental, physical health and a constructive home and community environment are important factors in giving birth to a healthy child. These factors influence the maternal, prenatal, and intrauterine environments and determine the overall state of the child according to the late psychologist Amos Wilson. Dr. Wilson also goes on to state: "In our effort to achieve maximum self actualization… we must not forget that the establishment of a healthy prenatal environment is the first and most important step to be taken in that direction."

One factor often overlooked is the participatory role of the father during pregnancy, the first true test for fatherhood. A man committed to the healthy birth of his child will provide unconditional love and support. He will see to it that the mother receives proper nutrition and other essential necessities. Her needs will not be taken lightly. Her nagging requests for some things is really the love and comfort she seeks in exchange for the suffering she must endure to bring a child in this world. A man's active role assures her that he is with her all the way. This helps her to maintain high levels of energy, assurance and peace of mind, all of which are necessities for a healthy newborn.

The education of a child is not primarily the responsibility of an institution (school). Education must be emphasized in the home. We must lay the foundation for a home program that motivates our children to do more reading, studying and creating. Children should be read to often in their earliest stages of development. The process should interchange as children develop their own reading/comprehensive abilities. Initial introduction to television and computers should be based solely on educational purposes. These viewing and interactive plays should be often monitored and carried out in a structured framework. It is extremely valuable to enforce proper hygiene, nutrition and studying principles. This will develop early discipline and harden into habit and tradition.

Communication must always be emphasized, encouraged and observed. Remember, there are all kinds of communication, i.e. appearance, attitude, doing things together, verbal conversation and or nonverbal body language. As a child develops effective communication skills, he or she will have a better relationship with life. We must refrain from always dictating and learn to listen to our children. It is the best way to understand how they perceive their world. This approach is what aids us in helping them to grow into a total person. Ethnic traditions, religious, cultural and or national holidays should be practiced in the homes. These family gathering should, at some point during the events, involve discussions around topics like: family, community life, and each child's future endeavor/responsibilities. For those who do not ascribe to traditional events, Sunday family gatherings should involve these important topics.

The extended family concept is vital to the home, especially where there is serious adult male absence. An extended male model should be present or implemented. As importantly, we must recapture our passion to struggle. We must imprint our values and principles upon the environmental activities and institutions that will also shape our children. The family is the first institution that set the pattern for socialization into the outside world. What a family practices in the home will reflect and determine the productivity of that family. But the power of environment can undermine the good intent of the home. Family traditions and belief systems should be inculcated into the various institutions that compose communities. When we examine strong communities we should discover strong families where the people of that community controls or has adequate input into their community institutions. If we are to empower our children then we must at least seek input into our community activities and institutions. We must stop expecting to raise sane children in an insane, deteriorating and hostile environment.

Lastly, our children must begin to see us, as parents/role models, manifest these ideas in the home and community. If we do not at least put forth a concerted effort to empower our children, then we really have no one else to blame but ourselves. What must be done to empower our children? We and only we must empower them. **Ourselves!**

RAINBOW COLORED CHILDREN

OH, MIGHTY RAINBOW COLORED BOYS
BLESSED BY THE SUN'S RAYS

YOU MUST RESPECT ALL WOMEN
THEY ARE PART OF THE WAY

TO IMPROVE THIS TROUBLED WORLD
THERE'S A PRICE YOU MUST PAY

MAKE IT PART OF YOUR DESTINY
THE WAY THE SUN IS PART OF DAY

MAKE THIS AFFIRMATION FOR THE BETTERMENT
OF THE WHOLE WORLD AS GOD'S NATION

*   *   *   *

OH, PRETTY RAINBOW COLORED GIRLS
KISSED BY THE SUN'S RAYS

HELP US IMPROVE THIS TROUBLED
WORLD, WE ARE STILL LED ASTRAY

USE YOUR LOVE, STRENGTH AND
WISDOW TO SHOW US THE WAY

PLEASE, ILLUMINATE OUR FUTURE SEED
THE WAY THE SUN DOES THE DAY

MAKE THIS AFFIRMATION FOR THE BETTERMENT
OF THE WHOLE WORLD AS GOD'S NATION

THIS OUTWARD FACIAL EXPRESSION IS NOT A PHOTO GIMMIC
EVERY WORD WE USE REFLECTS OUR OWN SELF-IMAGE

REMOVE THE "N-WORD" FROM YOUR VOCABULARY. IGNORANCE
BREEDS SELF-HATE, MENTAL ANGUISH AND INVISIBILE VIOLENCE

UNITED STATES SUPREME COURT
UNITED STATES OF AMERICA

AFRICAN-AMERICAN AWARENESS, INC.   x
                          PETITIONERS,

                                  x SUBJECT: THE WORD NIGGER
    -AGAINST-

                                  x   DOCKET#: 1555 - 2009

WHITE SUPREMACY, INC.
                       DEFENDANTS   x

THE UNITED STATES SUPREME COURT
(THE HIGHEST COURT IN THE LAND)

ORAL ARGUMENT

CHIEF JUSTICE: In the case at bar, the African-American Awareness, Inc., (henceforth, "petitioners") contend that White Supremacy, Inc., (henceforth, "defendants") should not be allowed to refer to them by the term nigger. The defendant argues that this claim is contradictory and therefore without merit and should be dismissed, since African-Americans have re-defined the term and now refer to themselves as niggers. This court has agreed to hear this case with respect to the question of usage. Both parties will be permitted a 10-minute oral argument. Counselor for petitioners, are you ready to proceed?

COUNSELOR FOR PETITIONERS: Yes, your honor. Thank you. The term nigger is a derogatory derivative from the Spanish word Negrear. It is pronounced in English as Negro or characterized as Negroid. The proper word Negroid is defined as an ethnic division of the human species regarding people of black, brown and even yellow pigmentation. But the word "nigger" was diabolically constructed/used by racist to justify their hatred and mistreatment against people of African descent. In earlier dictionaries this term referred to, "a dumb or ignorant person in reference to African-Americans." Today's dictionary defines the term as an offensive slang to members of Black-skinned people. Thus, the origin of the word in question is rooted in Africans-American suffering. It is reminiscent of deep psychological scares associated with overt acts of violence perpetuated by the decadences of these defendants upon Africans who were subjected to captivity (slavery).

Defendants attempt to seize the opportunity to make mockery of this ugly term filled with horrible memories because of its current usage by ignorant or uninformed African-Americans still suffering from an enslaved mentality is disadvantageous to the progress of our nation. It should be placed in American archives as a reminder of one of the most offensive words ever used in this country in reference to the harsh mistreatment of the American-American ethic group.

As a derogatory denotation the term should not be perceived as positive by way of connotation. The current effort to re-define and thus justify usage and acceptability of the N-word by ignorant Blacks (lay persons and/or professionals) only substantiates the profound and lingering affects of indoctrination that evolved out of the impact of psychological slavery. Nowhere in the esthetic validity of African-American culture defined by intellectual African-centered independent thinkers do we find a glorification of the term nigger justified.

To successfully transform African captive into American slaves, a systematized process had to be implemented. The enslavers deliberately prevented Africans from learning to read and write for the sole purpose of breeding ignorance. Degrading and intimidating terminology was also used as part of the enslavement process. The term nigger was enforced on African-Americans. A rejection of the term by what was considered a rebellious slave or freeman almost always resulted in punishment carried out in the presence of other Blacks. (See: Roots v. Slavery, 57 S. Ct. 1227) This form of punishment was designed to inject and to instill fear in the minds and hearts of other Blacks who refused to accept their defined status as ignorantly subservient and worthless captives in the eyes of their oppressors.

Imagine being forced to respond to this negative term or be punished for your refusal. Moreover, African-American children witnessing their parents and elders obediently responding to this term when spoken to by the enslavers. Although this was many of their ways of preventing punishment, it served to plant into the tiny brains of generations of children born into this kind of arrangement a perception of who they must be. The N-word went from being an acceptable term by Blacks in response to their masters to Blacks referring to each other as niggers. When you strip a people of their identity, forcibly inject them with self-hatred, you create a confused people. (See: Exhibit A)

Today, most African-Americans and Americans of all ethnicities are sensitively opposed to the word in question relative to their rejection because of the memories it holds to connect us to a horrible past. It echoes the vicious murders, rapes and tortures of African-Americans. "Nigger" was the loudest outcry of hatred expressed by racist who murdered, brutalized and terrorized during many of our nation's past and even present atrocities. (See: Exhibit M) For many African-Americans, particularly during the rise of the Klu Klux Klan that word confirmed the defining moment of death. Many Blacks were forced to carry that diabolical term with them into horrible deaths as they struggled for their last breath of life. Because of these tribulations, Blacks and progressive elements of our society have pursued a long history of demonstrations, litigation and legislation to do away with mistreatment. It is important to note, petitioners are aggressively engaged in educating ignorant Blacks still suffering from the effects of this enslaved mentality. (See: Exhibit N-T)

Justices of the court, petitioners understand you have agreed to hear this case with respect to the question of usage. But that question cannot be answered out of context with the historical implication associated with African-American suffering. Petitioners believes these few example, supported by documents and other moving papers, now before the court, will give substance to satisfy the courts need to put to rest this ugly term. However, to deny this petition would be to endorse linguistic discrimination and erase away our nation's commitment to the many amendments upheld by our constitution. Petitioners ask that this court not allow defendants to make mockery out of past struggles associated with deep unhealed wounds tied to the African-American historical experience. Thank you, your honorable chief justice and justices of the court.

CHIEF JUSTICE: You are welcome counselor. Counselor for defendants, are you ready to proceed?

COUNSELOR FOR DEFENDANTS: Yes I am, your honor. Defendants have also submitted numerous documents to support its contention. Thus, we intend to make oral argument brief. Defendants agree, in part, with petitioners assertion concerning past psychological linguistic assault on petitioner's ethnicity. Initially, this may have been attributed to past enslavement and evolved out of racial discrimination. Because of full freedom now enjoyed by all members of our society, petitioners have opportunities far beyond those conditions of past enslavement. (See: Exhibit A- F) Not only are African-Americans enjoying the benefits of education, this group has excelled in every aspect of life so much so that there is now an African-American on the United States Supreme Court and even an African-American as President of the United States. They have and continue to contribute to the betterment of our great nation. They are hardly slaves! More specifically, the argument that the term nigger is a bloody word used by ignorant blacks is unfounded. Usage of this term by professional blacks in the areas of music, comedy, athletes, business, etc, is well documented and extends far beyond the boundaries of ignorance. (See: Exhibit H–I) In the past, one gentleman went on nightline to argue the term as justifiably while other Blacks went on various talk shows also attempting to justify its usage. (See: Exhibit J – N)

Justices of the court, Black experts argued that the African-American expression and re-definition of the English language is based on their own unique connotation. They have referenced it as an Ebonics interpretation of spoken English and argued that Ebonics should be taught in predominately black public and private schools. Could this be why they find no disrespect in calling their own women and little girls, "bitches, holes, hoochies and hood rats," while at the same time, using Ebonics to define their attraction for white women with terms like; "pink toes, Blondie and snow bunnies?" Of course, all women are beautiful! But petitioner's Ebonics would not be a cause for litigation against defendants if defendants were to adopt petitioner's negative terminology for white women. The hidden meaning behind their use of language tells us that the effort to use past oppression as an excuse is unjustifiably.

To charge defendants and not other groups or African-Americans themselves, who use the term, invalidates this claim and renders it as a form of targeted grouping or reverse discrimination. Defendant also agrees, the question before this court should not be the issue of usage of the word nigger. The real question is, how come defendants are the only ones being tried? To single our defendants, over other ethnic groups, especially African-Americans themselves, for using the term is clearly discriminatory. (Emphasis added)!

Today, common usage of the word nigger by petitioners has both negative and positive implications. Thus, defendant's usage cannot be assumed negative. African-Americans who have argued in favor of the term does so with the proposition that it means something positive, i.e., "my brother or my man." However, there are some blacks that use the word nigger negatively. Our prisons are filled with them, killing, raping and destroying themselves. Just like in the case of their ancestors "nigger" was the last thing echoes by many victims of their own kind, e.g., "kill that bitch ass nigger; shoot that fucking' nigger, now. (Pow, Pow, Pow, etc.) !"

Defendants do not have to make mockery out of the word nigger. If that is their intentions, defendants can get a greater pleasure listening and watching African-Americans make mockery out of it themselves. Isn't it ironic how petitioners show a lesser concern for addressing issues like: black-on-black crime or black purchasing power exploitation. There are members of the African-American group who have made a choice to glorify criminality and their own self-hatred through language using music, magazines, etc., as a vehicle. To charge the defendants with usage of the term nigger would be like petitioners now charging the defendants with slander for exposing these facts.

In light of the facts presented in this case, it is obvious that African-Americans have re-defined the word nigger with no personal sympathy, or shame. By doing so, the petitioners historical chains of slavery argument looses it validity and the case presented before this court looses its aim. It would be contradictory for this court to hold, the defendant, who now claim, usage of the word as an African-American connotative preference with blame.

Petitioners as an ethnicity have obviously separated themselves from their historical atrocities by mere usage of the N-word out of which they maintain is the result of being trained. We are sure that the court will agree that any group of people operating with integrity would never associate themselves with a term reminiscence of so much pain. But to re-define such a term, as a self-conscious choice, is like someone not following the rules but still wanting to play the game. Therefore, this court should have not other alternative but to conclude, because there are still African-Americans who refer to themselves as niggers, it is appropriate to determine that defendants are within their rights to assume that petitioners have changed their name.

It is inappropriate to single out the defendants just because petitioners alleged that defendants have bias views. Note that the issue of usage would be properly before this court if it involved African-Americans as petitioners (those who totally reject the term) -against- African-Americans as defendants (those who connotatively use the term).

In conclusion, to accuse defendants of using the term nigger as mockery when, it is commonly accepted by many Blacks themselves, would be to use defendants as an escape goat for their own folly. As long as petitioners call themselves niggers they have no claim. Therefore, this case is without merit and should be dismissed. Thank you your honor and justices of the court.

CHIEF JUSTICE: You are welcome, counselor. The court has just heard oral arguments by both parties. We will consider your presentations and review all materials submitted by both sides. A decision will be rendered by the Honorable Keith Tyrone Bush, Chief Justice of the United States Supreme Court, within 90-days. That will be all gentlemen.

COUNSELOR FOR THE DEFENDANTS: Thank you your honor.

COUNSELOR FOR THE PETITIONERS: Thank you very much your honor.

TRIBUTE TO THE COMRADES

MAY I SHARE SOME WITH YOU:

The spark of life animates humanity into motion; stimulates the thought process in order to bring forth the reality of the soul. Humanity has captured the spark and harnessed its potential, channeling it into fire that flames a civilization. But how civilized is man when he places other men and women inside a cage like an animal... colonizing their thoughts, shackling their tongue, making them self-abusive and destructive. We must intensify the heat of our desire to be free by igniting the powerful explosive vapors of determination lingering deep within the depths of our souls. Lets bring forth a new reality!

Aka "Lord Amsu"

When any person treats you badly, or speaks ill of you, remember that he or she acts or speaks from an impression that it is right for them to do so. Now, it is not possible that they should follow what appears right to you, but only what appears so to them selves. Therefore, if they judge from false appearance, they are the ones hurt; since they too are the ones deceived. For if any person takes a true proposition to be false, the proposition of truth is not hurt, but only the person is deceived. Henceforth than, setting out from these principles, you will meekly bear with a person who unduly reviles you: For you will say upon every such action, "It seemed so to them."

Aka "Saint Lawrence"

Life is worth living for and life is worth dying for! The question you and I must ask ourselves; whose life are we willing to live and die for? Is it for the life of those who continue to oppress us and forever hold us in the grip of bondage and ignorance? Will it be for the life of justice and equality, the right to be self-determining, the right to live in peace and harmony with our children and the ones yet to come. The choice is yours! I already made my choice; I will live and die to be free!

Aka "Jamel Baruti Bakari"

Despite bias forces, debilitating social conditions or devastating consequences... the conquest for freedom must be vigorous (24-7) for our chemistry is threatened from sun-up to sun-up. Inmost, the practice of self-awareness, self-determination and self-sufficiency must be implanted in each present and descending generation. Whereas, those who remain sincere and authentic with the struggle, in the eyes of the slave ship, must manifest the power of fire!!! Remember, in our domain we shall carry no dead weight; except that of the lifeless betrayal-like... to the volcano...

Aka "Waki"

History reconnects us to our roots. A tree without roots is dead, and people who do not know their history, likewise, are dead. They cannot dig deep into the past and extract from it that which will enable them to grow into a strong nation... That is why history is so important. It provides us with the knowledge and understanding we need to place our existence and our purpose in perspective. It gives us a positive, definite base from which to work, in order that we might chart a more careful and correct course for the future. It has been said that history is a weapon that can be used for a people's good and advancement, or against them for their own destruction. The choice is ours!

Aka "Cushmere"

THE VISITOR

HE ENTERED MY HOME IN THE STILL OF THE NIGHT
NOT MAKING A SOUND OR SHOWING A LIGHT;

A SPECTRAL FIGURE STATELY AND BOLD;
WITH LUMINOUS EYES PIERCING MY SOUL.

HE SLOWLY APPROACHED ME AND SAT ON MY BED;
AND WITHOUT HESITATION HERE'S WHAT HE SAID:

I'VE WATCHED YOU MY BROTHER THROUGH ALL OF MY YEARS;
I'VE SEEN YOU IN BLISS, I'VE SEEN YOU IN TEARS.
I'VE SEEN YOU REPENT TO THE GREAT ONE ABOVE
I'VE SEEN YOU MAKE MOCKERY OF THOSE WHOM YOU LOVE

     *   *   *   *   *

YOU WORSHIPPED YOUR MASTER AND THOUGHT YOU WERE COOL;
AND WOULDN'T ACCEPT YOU WERE MERELY A TOOL.

AND NOW THAT YOU BATTERED YOUR HEAD UNTIL IT'S NUMB,
WHAT WILL YOU DO WITH THE YEARS YET TO COME?

WITH THIS LAST QUESTION HE AROSE AND WAS GONE;
AND I STOOD THERE THINKING FOR GOD KNOWS HOW LONG.

WHO WAS THAT GREAT MAN WHO CAME OUT OF THE GLOOM;
DISTURBING MY SLUMBER, INVADING MY ROOM?

     *   *   *   *   *

AND THROUGH A HAZE, I SAW HIS FACE GRIN:

HE SAID: **MY NAME IS MALCOLM X, THE MAN YOU SHOULD HAVE BEEN!**

BY: Aka "NYIKA"

THANKSGIVING

NO THANKS PILGRIM SETTLERS   **I WILL NOT FEAST WITH YOU**

NOT IN FORGETFULNESS FOR THE VICIOUS,
VICIOUS SLAUGHTER OF **THE RED PEOPLE,**
THUS KIND ENOUGH TO TEACH
YOU HOW TO SURVIVE

NO THANKS PILGRIM SETTLERS   **I WILL NOT FEAST WITH YOU**

NEVER AGAIN WILL I EAT OFF OF THE BONES
OF MY FOREPARENTS HIDDEN IN TURKEY MEAT,
SMILING PUMPKINS SYMBOLIZING THE BEAST, ON WET
BLOODY TABLES DECORATED WITH KLAN SHEETS

NOR WILL I TASTE ONE DROP FROM THOSE DIRTY CUPS
FILLED TO THE TOP, CONCOCTED WITH AFRICAN SWEAT,
BLOOD AND TEARS. TO YOU, IT'S A BEAUTIFUL DREAM
TO ME, IT'S A HORRIBLE, HORRIBLE NIGHTMARE

NO THANKS PILGRIM SETTLERS   **I WILL NOT FEAST WITH YOU**

IT'S LIKE THE RIGHTEOUS GIVING THANKS TO SATAN
OVER GOD, WHOM THEY HAVE ALL LOST THEIR FAITH IN

AFRICAN PEOPLE GIVING THANKS TO APARTHEID
OR NATIVE AMERICANS REJOICING IN MASS
MURDER, RAPE AND MENTAL GENOCIDE

NO VICTIM GIVES THANKS TO THEIR ROBBERS
THUS THANKSGIVING I WILL GIVE TO MY
OWN FORE MOTHERS & FATHERS

NO THANKS PILGRIM SETTLERS   **I WILL NOT FEAST WITH YOU**

JUBILEE TO ALL OF MY ANCESTORS NO LONGER LIVING
A CELEBRATION FOR ALL OF YOUR GIVING

A DAY I WILL HARAMBEE IN FEAST
PAY TO YOU TRIBUTE & PEACE

FOR SHOWING ME THE WAY, FOR
OPENING THE PATH TO A
NEW BRIGHTER DAY

"TO MY ANCESTORS THIS FEAST IS FOR YOU"

UMOJA KARAMU   **UMOJA KARAMU**
                 UMOJA KARAMU

REMEMBER: EVERY FOURTH SUNDAY IN NOVEMBER

        *   *   *   *

NOTE:

TO MAKE MY THANKSGIVING A PERSONAL
ANCESTRAL DEDICATION IS NOT BASED ON HATE,

I LOOKED TO THE PAST AS A REMINDER THAT IT IS
TO MY ANCESTORS WHO SACRFICED SO MUCH

AND SINCE THANKSGIVING MEANS TO GIVE THANKS,
ON THIS DATE (THE 4TH SUNDAY IN NOVEMBER)

TO YOU I CELEBRATE !

IT'S TIME TO WAKE UP FROM THE NIGHTMARE

LIES IN YOUR MINDS, YOUR BRAINS ARE DROWNING IN PUS
WEAK AND MADE CORRUPTED, MISGUIDED, SELF-DESTRUCTIVE
DYING FROM DISEASE, SELF-HATRED AND THAT INTOXICATED STUFF

ABUSED AND CONFUSED WITH NO ONE TO TRUST
CHAINS AROUND YOUR BRAINS AND YOU'RE LOSING YOUR TOUCH
SUFFERING FOR HUNDREDS OF YEARS, IT'S MORE THAN ENOUGH

THE SAME GAME THE NAME WAS CHANGED, FROM CHATTEL CHAINS TO HANDCUFFS

IT'S A STRUGGLE! IT'S INSANE! AND YOU STILL WON'T STAND-UP
IT'S A SHAME EACH TIME YOU CLAIM, "I AIN'T WITH THAT BLACK STUFF"
BUT WHEN IT COMES TO HUSTLING CRACK MONEY, THEN YOU GET TOUGH
THAT ALONE SHOULD TELL YOU, SOMETHING IS WRONG WITH US

WE NEED RESPECT, LOVE AND POWER, WE ALSO NEED THE DOLLAR
ITS TIME WE DO FOR SELF INSTEAD OF BEGGING SO MUCH
EXPLOITATION, DISRESPECT AND PERVERSION OF LUST
TURNING GIRLS INTO WOMEN BY THE GROWTH OF THEIR
BREASTS AND THE SIZE OF THEIR BUTTS

NOW OUR CHILDREN HAVING BABIES IN THE HOOD LIFE IS CRAZY
STARVING, ROBBING, RAPING, KILLING, LIVING UNJUST
HEARTS FROZED COLD, HEAD READY TO BUST

IT'S TIME TO WAKE UP FROM THE NIGHTMARE

FEAR

WHAT'S WORSE THAN A SINGLE SPERM'S ABILITY
TO SURVIVE WHILE MILLIONS DIE – IN A DEADLY
RAIN STORM DRIPPING DOWN THE WALLS OF THE WOMB

TO TRIUMPHANTLY REACH DESTINY, HENCEFORTH,
"THE SPARK OF LIFE" EVOLVING FROM ONE INTO
BILLIONS OF CELLS - COMPOSING A MIRACULOUS ORGANISM

TO MANIFEST AN EXISTENCE JUST ONCE IN THIS
BEAUTIFUL PLACE CALLED PHYSICAL REALITY

- ONLY TO DISCOVER -

YOU HAVE ENTERED INTO A WORLD
WHERE YOUR LIFE WILL BE LIVED
AS A SERVANT TO ANOTHER

BECAUSE:

IN THE WOMB, IT WAS STRUGGLE THAT BROUGHT YOU HERE,
BUT IN THE PHYSICAL WORLD, YOU WILL LIVE YOUR ONLY
LIFE AS A SLAVE, IF YOU KEEP LIVING IT IN FEAR!

GLOSSARY

AMEN RA: A Kemetic (Egyptian) representation of the sun in the form of a deity. Amen reigns over the invisible (also meaning hidden), while Ra represents God (the life force energy of the visible world).

BA-HUTI: An African people with a hereditary stature of five to six feet tall. They are the original inhabitants of Southern African.

BA-TUSI: An African people with a hereditary stature of six feet or taller. They are the original inhabitants of Southern African.

BA-TWA: An African people with a hereditary stature of four to five feet. They are the original inhabitants of Southern African.

DANKANESH: A fossil discovered in Africa and is believed to be one of the worlds oldest (approximately 150,000 years). She is widely known as "Lucy." The Ethiopians called her Dankanesh which means, "She is wonderful."

KHNEMU: A Kemetic Ram-headed god who is said to have created man from clay on a potter's wheel.

KHUWILAND: The great lake regions of Central and Southern Africa referred to as the birthplace of humanity.

LUVMERIZED: Someone mesmerized by love.

LUV-TRAYAL: Someone betrayed under the pretense of love.

MAAT: The highest Kemetic moral principle upon which the divine order of creation rest. Maat is truth, justice, harmony and right action. To live in accord with Maat is the rewards of a just life.

UMOJA KARAMU: Umoja is a Swahili word that means "unity" in the English language. Karamu is a Swahili word for "feast."